INVESTING SIMPLIFIED

A Guide to Financial Freedom for Busy Professionals

JAGANMOHAN REDDY A.

ISBN 979-8-89026-492-3

Table of Contents

Introduction

If you don't find a way to make money while you sleep, you will work until you Die

—Warren Buffett

Congratulations on taking the first step towards achieving financial freedom. This book is about building long-term wealth for working professionals who are busy with their day-jobs and want to invest passively on a regular basis. If someone starts working in their 20s, there is a 30+ year time horizon for wealth-building and this book will focus on building wealth over this period with minimal time and effort and without deep knowledge of investing.

This book is for career professionals like IT professionals, doctors, engineers, chartered accountants, lawyers, architects, interior and fashion designers, artistes in the TV/movie industry, media professionals and anyone who works full-time to earn money. As a career professional, you need to spend most, if not all, of your energy to do well in your respective professions apart from family responsibilities and social life. In these modern times with "work-from-home", our days are already filled with work and life and it is very difficult to have another major time-consuming activity in our lives. While you are busy with your job and family, the book aims to help your savings work for you over the long term.

Traditionally, fixed deposits (FDs) are considered the best for saving money, which is a huge myth. They provide limited fixed returns, but when you add taxes and inflation to those returns, you are not growing your wealth at all and in fact, your purchasing power is going down over time with fixed deposits.

This book will show you how to build wealth over the long term with minimum effort and risk. It will introduce you to new concepts of investing that are not well-known in mainstream investing and help you build your conviction in these methods. It will introduce you to the concept of portfolios, stocks and bonds, indexing and Systematic Investment Plans (SIPs). It will also introduce you to real estate strategies for long-term wealth creation and talk about strategies for combining the stock market and real estate for building long-term wealth. These methods are proven universally in the US, India and other growing economies and they work for any career professional who does not have the time to understand the nitty-gritty details of stock picking, is willing to take limited risk and has the ability to hold the investment for the long term.

The purpose of writing this book is to share the author's learnings and experiences. Like the author, most career professionals have not learned personal finance management during their education. They make mistakes during the initial days of their earning period and lose everything they had earned in the first five years.

The author strongly believes that personal finance should be a part of our education system, introducing basic concepts of personal finance management and investing. Interestingly, it is not part of the education curriculum in many countries. It is crucial to make money as a career professional, but it is equally important to learn how to make those savings work for us over the long term. The only way to achieve financial freedom is to build wealth over time, which will provide a fixed income to replace your salary.

Having graduated without any understanding of financial management, I started playing with the stock market in the US in 1998, investing in great Tech companies of that time like Microsoft, Cisco and a few other new startups like Amazon, eBay and many others. It was a fantastic run for two years, where I got 5x returns within two years. With the way things were going, I felt I would be close to retirement in another two years, reaching my million-dollar ambition at that time in January 2000.

What followed in the next few months was like a lightning strike from the sky: I lost almost all my wealth in the next nine months and ended up with loans to cover my losses. It was a rude shock that took me three months to accept the reality and my mistakes of investing in the stock market without any understanding. Then, I went into a lot of soul-searching to find out what went wrong. I spent the next six months researching about investing and I realized that I was just shooting in the dark without any understanding of my investments in the stock market.

Since then, I have done a lot of reading, with a focus on making the stock market work for a common man or someone with a busy day job. I have used these learnings over the last 20 years of my life and created wealth over time to achieve my financial freedom. In this book, I am going to share these learnings at different stages of life with a clear actionable plan for you.

The book is also for those who have significant wealth and want to grow it with less risk and less time. This approach has been employed by many wealthy Western families over the years and with Indians growing wealth, it is important for everyone to understand these concepts well. These concepts are not very popular in mainstream finance as they go against the interests of the financial industry and media.

This book will introduce you to basic concepts of personal finance, which are constant and limited compared to the depth of knowledge required for successful stock investments. The concepts to be introduced in this book are contrary to everything you hear in the news every day and different from what most people do around us daily. To give a simple analogy from cricket, this book will help you to hire Virat Kohli for free to play for you, rather than playing cricket against Virat Kohli trying to win. You know that it is not smart to play against Virat trying to win, but that is what most stock investors do every day in the stock market.

This book introduces you to building wealth over the long term without demanding two of your most valuable resources:

1. Time: You are not focused on the stock market's ups and downs on a daily basis. Watching and reacting to market ups and downs every day will

surely create health issues like BP or sugar more than creating wealth.

2. Depth of Knowledge: You can focus on building skills for your primary career instead of learning about stocks and daily movements in the stock market.

These principles helped me personally and a group of friends around me to build long-term personal wealth. It helped me recover the money I lost in the 2000 *"dot com"* bust and made more money in the stock market over the long term with less time and knowledge. The most challenging thing was staying put with these principles while there was a lot of noise in the news about the market, like the 2007/2008 financial crisis, the housing bust and the recent COVID crash in markets in March 2020. You need to understand, own and digest these principles and do your research to believe them with strong conviction. I strongly encourage you to read this book and it will be the biggest investment return of your time and money for a lifetime. It is a promise!

Part I: Career Professional and Financial Freedom

"Financial freedom does not mean retiring from work, but rather having the ability to make decisions about how and where we allocate our time and energy without being constrained by finances."

Two friends grew up together in a small town and went their separate ways at the age of 21 to pursue their careers. They reunited 30 years later and shared their life stories. Despite both working hard in their chosen careers and earning almost equal salaries, one friend had realized the importance of saving and investing early on, while the other only came to this realization later in life. As they discussed their plans for retirement, their stories were vastly different. One had accumulated enough wealth to retire comfortably, while the other was forced to work throughout retirement due to financial needs. Although they made similar incomes, the difference in their financial freedom was significant due to the early savings and investments of one friend.

This scenario is likely relatable to many people and the book aims to guide career professionals towards achieving financial freedom. In this section of the book, the concept of financial freedom is defined, its importance is explained and a long-term wealth-building strategy is presented.

Financial freedom may have different meanings for different people. It can be defined as achieving a specific financial goal, such as a net worth of **X** crores, which would allow one to pursue their passions without financial constraints or rewards. Another way to think about it is having a parallel income that covers one's financial needs, enabling them to focus on their passions without being burdened by mortgage payments and family expenses.

As we progress in our careers, expenses tend to increase at a much faster pace than salaries. Starting with marriage, car and new home, expenses extend to children's education, among other things. Investing in passive income or wealth creation is necessary to meet increasing expenses and achieve financial freedom early in life.

Successful businesses that are listed in the stock market create most of the wealth. Individuals like Bill Gates, Steve Jobs, Narayana Murthy and Ambani feature on the rich lists of various countries. However, for every successful company, there are likely more than 100 failures, making it a challenging task and not suited for everyone.

Career professions such as IT, Medicine, Law and Accounting require significant time and effort, coupled with family responsibilities. With the speed of life and limited time, it can be challenging to keep up with professional changes. For example, the software industry is rapidly evolving, with changes in cloud computing, AI and big data. Staying up-to-date with technological advances is crucial for a successful career and specialization is the key in the digital world. It can be challenging to devote time and attention to the stock market on a daily basis, given the demanding needs of a modern-day career.

Chapter 1: Career Professional

Imagine a future where your money works for you 24x7 while you are enjoying your time with family, on a beach, or working on things you are passionate about. As a career professional, you are likely to go through a 40+ hour busy workweek. A report by the National Sample Survey Office (NSSO) shows that workers in Indian cities are working an average of 53 to 54 hours a week. Over the last two decades, working hours have increased for professionals in India.

In this rapidly changing technological world, almost all professions require continuous education to keep up-to-date with technology and business changes. As an IT professional, for example, you need to stay abreast of all the technological changes such as cloud, big data and machine learning. As a doctor, you need to stay ahead of medical advances and technology's role in medicine. You need to continuously educate yourself in your field of specialization. As a lawyer, you need to continuously adapt to using technology for historical judgements and interpretation of the law. There is no field or professional which is not impacted by technology. Very few exceptions are labour-intensive and unskilled jobs which are paying less and less overtime with automation.

As our jobs demand more than 100% of our time, focus and energy, we need to find a way to make our money work for us. Obviously, it requires saving money from our salary in a systematic way and investing in a way to protect the capital and grow it over the long term. Assuming you start working at 21, you have almost 40+ years to build this wealth over the long term.

Starting early gives you a big advantage due to the compounding nature of wealth-building. It is super important to start as early as you can and it is never too late to start. To give a specific example, if you start saving a fixed amount X using these principles from age 25 to 40 (**15 years**) and your friend does from 35 to 65 (**30 years**) for the same amount X, **your portfolio amount at 65 years of age will be more than 30% higher than your friend**. Notice that you saved half the amount compared to your friend but the final balance is 30% higher than your friend's. That is the power of compounding and the principles of this simple investing philosophy.

It is very important to align our thoughts and behaviours to the outcomes we want in life. There are people around us who keep telling us that money is bad, rich are heartless, etc. First, get out of the confusion (if there is any) on whether you want to make money or not. Money is neither good nor bad and it is only your relationship with money that defines good or bad. We see many people with a bad relationship with money. We all must realize that money is one of the most important things in life. One thing that comes ahead of money is personal relationships, but both are not exclusive. We all should strive to make money and have great relationships with people around us.

As career professionals, usually, we all have goals on where we want to be five years from now in terms of designation, influence, or salary. But most of us don't have the same goals for our finances. Many times, it comes to our mind but we keep postponing it for various reasons. Either we do not have the knowledge, don't know where to start, or are generally not interested in understanding the topic. Sometimes we don't do it because we know it requires some difficult steps like saving money from our existing salary which may impact our current lifestyle. But it is important to dream about our ideal financial future and take effective steps from today to realize that dream.

Understanding the purpose of money in our lives and having conviction about it is important. Many of us dream of retiring from full-time, stressful work by age 40 or 50 to focus on other interests. However, time flies and before we know it, we've reached our 50s. Long-term wealth creation is the best way to realize this dream, rather than winning a random lottery. Time is a major factor that works in our favour when we start our careers. Although we may have a lower initial salary due to loans, etc., it's essential to start the habit of saving as early as possible and build discipline around saving money every month.

The strategies and actions suggested in this book aim to create a financial foundation for families to achieve basic financial independence. However, it doesn't limit what else you can do in life. This investment approach will build the foundation to give you the freedom to explore new opportunities in life. For example, if you're interested in starting a business in your 30s, you need this basic financial freedom approach to explore that. Otherwise, you'll always be tied down by monthly expenses or the investment required to start the business.

Whatever your plans are for the later part of your career, this book will help you create the financial foundation required to reach your goals. It emphasizes the importance of saving early and investing in the stock market without deep knowledge to help you build wealth.

Chapter 2: Financial Freedom Defined

"A good financial plan is a road map that shows us exactly how the choices we make today will help our financial needs of tomorrow."

At some point in our lives, we all aspire to reach a stage where money does not control or dictate how we spend our time and energy. This depends on whether we work for money or make money and wealth work for us. Money is a bad master but an excellent servant and we always want to be the master controlling it. As we continue to work full-time, we need to have a plan in place to build long-term wealth for money to become our servant. Many of us have different passions, such as travelling, farming, helping the needy, painting, music and many others. As we work in our fields, leveraging the expertise we have developed over time, we are also helping society as engineers, doctors and lawyers and we are making our living.

To raise a family and enjoy life's comforts, like cars and apartments, will keep us very focused for 30 to 40 years.

In parallel, we need to build a financial roadmap to build wealth and achieve financial freedom. It is a dream for many career professionals to achieve financial independence as early as possible in their careers. Please note that this is not the same as retirement; it is only about freedom from money. When we have financial freedom, our time and energy are not tied to money and we may decide to continue what we do because we love our work or try new areas of interest. The key point is the freedom from money for us to spend our time and energy anywhere we want.

The Value of Money

It is super important to have clarity on the role money plays in our lives. We need to understand the balance between running after money and earning enough money for our financial freedom. Traditionally in our societies, money is projected as a bad thing and elders keep telling us not to get into the trap of money. It is true to some extent when people forget that money is not the end but only a means to live our lives with freedom. Financial freedom is about us stopping thinking about money so we can focus on other important things in life. We also hear that money can't solve all problems in life. It is true, but money can solve all our money problems. We need to be clear in our minds about the importance of financial freedom and why we want to earn it. It is super important to have clarity on this important aspect of financial freedom. We all know money in itself is neither good nor bad. It all depends on how we use it as a means for our life goals. We all know that money alone can't buy mental peace, health or relationships, but we also know that it can solve many of our life problems like a house, car, vacation, kids' education, marriage and all necessary things and luxuries in life.

Inflation

Inflation refers to the rise in the prices of most goods and services of daily or common use, such as food, clothing and housing, among others. As investors, we need to fight against inflation to have returns higher than inflation to build wealth. Let us understand this with an example. Let's say we can buy a sofa for Rs.15,000 today and the same sofa costs Rs. 20,000 after five years due to inflation. If we invest the same 15,000 rupees today and it becomes Rs. 20,000 (after tax) after five years, it means inflation has eaten up our returns and our net investment return is zero. We need to find an investment vehicle that will beat inflation after all expenses and taxes. When we think about financial freedom, understanding this concept is very important to ensure that our freedom from money sustains for the rest of our lives.

Financial Freedom: What It Means and How to Achieve It

Financial freedom can be interpreted in different ways by different people. For some, it means accumulating investable wealth that would give them the confidence to live off the returns from their net worth and feel independent. For others, it means having a parallel source of income that can cover their living expenses almost equivalent to their salary.

There are different routes to achieving financial freedom and some of them are detailed below:

The first route is through entrepreneurship. This involves identifying and solving a big problem impacting many and building a business around it. Successful entrepreneurship creates wealth for the business owner, employees and stakeholders. However, this path requires a 360-degree understanding of business, full-time commitment and initial investment to start the business. Not everyone can take this route, as it is a difficult road and not meant for the faint-hearted. Examples of successful entrepreneurs include Dhirubhai Ambani, who started Reliance with limited investment and grew it into a big business in India and Bill Gates and Steve Jobs, who founded Microsoft and Apple respectively, in the 70s. Recently, we have seen examples of Flipkart, PayTM in India and Amazon, Uber and Tesla in the USA. While the idea of starting an entrepreneurial journey is exciting, it is essential to understand that for every successful company, there are over 100+ failures in India. Therefore, it is important to be aware of the challenges and founder's journey before taking the leap.

The second route is for salaried employees and working professionals. This route involves two elements. First, you need to build skills that make you employable and enable you to earn a good salary every month. The second part is about planning your salary in a way that helps you build wealth over the long term. As working professionals, most of us do well on the first part but find it challenging to execute the second part. The investing world is complex and many times we end up making the wrong choices. To simplify this, you don't need to invest and make money in every vehicle out there like stocks, real estate, gold, insurance, PPF, etc. Instead, focus on fundamentals and get over the fear of missing out.

In conclusion, financial freedom is achievable through different routes, but it requires a clear understanding of your goals and a well-defined plan of action. Whether you choose the entrepreneurship or the salaried employee route, it is important to be patient, persistent and disciplined in your approach to achieving financial freedom.

Here is the simple formula for building wealth as a salaried employee:

- Set up an automated SIP (Systematic Investment Plan) every month. The amount invested should be based on personal choice and financial situation.

- Understand the power of compounding and indexing. Surround yourself with friends who believe in this philosophy and talk about it to maintain your conviction.

- Stay away from the noise of individual stocks and market predictions by pundits.

- Avoid the temptation to sell or time the market when the stock market starts crashing.

You will see the magic happen in a couple of years. You don't need to understand much, but you need to have conviction in this methodology and execute it. This process is against common sense, which makes it difficult to practise. Although I have had this conviction for the last 20 years, I have tried to time the market twice with small amounts. While this is not bad, it demonstrates the difficulty of practising it. This is where a group of friends talking about this really helps with executing the plan.

Some of us take the investing route where we already have some wealth inherited from our parents. You can invest this money in real estate and build wealth over the long run. If you are fortunate enough to inherit wealth from your parents, you can focus on investing this wealth across different assets like stocks, real estate and monthly yielding assets like rental properties. You can continue this route with full-time or part-time investing and achieve financial freedom over time.

Stock market investing with a good understanding and depth of knowledge on value investing is another option. The best book on this topic is "Intelligent Investor" by Ben Graham, the guru of Warren Buffet. This option is for everyone who is not in the first two categories. The good thing about the stock market is that you can be part-time and start with small investments, unlike real estate. We will discuss different ways to invest in the stock market in the following chapter.

Chapter Summary/Key Takeaways: Creating personal wealth over time can be achieved in different ways based on your situation and interest. The entrepreneurial path to solving a real-world problem and building a business around it is the most common way to build wealth quickly. The world's wealthiest people, such as Bill Gates, Steve Jobs and Jeff Bezos, have made their fortunes this way. However, this path is very difficult with a low success ratio and requires an initial investment. Investing inherited wealth in real estate or other assets that yield monthly income is another way to achieve financial freedom. Stock market investing is another common way to create wealth and works well for full-time professionals, as it requires small investment capital to start with and can be done alongside your job. In the next chapter, we will discuss different ways of stock market investment for creating wealth.

Chapter 3:
Indian Investing Patterns and Opportunities

Why Do 95% of Indians Invest Only in Physical Assets?

Historically, India has been a socialist economy until liberalization began in 1991 under then Prime Minister PV Narasimha Rao. Most of our parents and older generations are comfortable with traditional assets such as gold, real estate and fixed deposits (FDs) and were not exposed to the stock market until the 1990s. The stock market was often viewed as a risky and gambling-based investment option, associated with scams and minimal wealth creation before the 1990s. Government bonds and FDs provided nearly a 10% return, which worked well for our parents' generation. However, with economic liberalization, the interest rates have declined and inflation has increased. This investment pattern is no longer effective for the current generation in their 30s and 40s. With FD returns at 6%, barely meeting inflation and not growing wealth, it is crucial for this generation to move away from traditional physical assets or FDs and transition to stock market investment with a conservative approach.

Although valid fears associated with the stock market exist, such as daily fluctuations in investment value and past scams like Harshad Mehta in the 1990s and market crashes in 2000, 2007/2008, it is necessary to invest in the stock market. Liberalization enabled many businesses to grow and create wealth in the stock market. Investing in the stock market requires specialist knowledge to analyse the stock/company or research the right mutual fund manager. However, investment advisers are not always necessary with the investment strategies explained in this book. The primary goal is to simplify investment to such an extent that individuals can manage their investments with a couple of hours a year while focusing on career growth.

Simplifying investment is the most important goal of this book. Except for investing professionals, most of us are not much interested in investing, other than the need to grow our wealth. The complexity of this space with all kinds of jargon meant for finance experts leaves the common man with two options: research and trust someone like an investment adviser with their money or keep saved money in FDs or physical assets like gold or real estate out of fear of the stock market.

The share of stock market equities in the form of direct stocks, mutual funds and others has increased from 2.7% to 4.8% of the household balance sheet in March 2022. This increase is a positive sign, but it is still relatively very small compared to other investment options. For example, FDs are still three times the equities and physical assets like property and gold are still 64% of the household balance sheet. In comparison, 50% of US households invested in the stock market as of March 2020.

Chapter Summary/Key Takeaways: As India's economy continues to grow, there is a significant opportunity to create wealth in the Indian stock market in the long run. The Indian economy is at a place where the US stock market was in the 1960s. Therefore, it is crucial to understand and learn simple ways to participate in the Indian stock market to grow wealth.

Chapter 4:
Personal Finance Basics

Personal finance can often be complicated and overwhelming, with various definitions and understandings in the financial industry. However, these complex ideas don't necessarily benefit the average person who may not have a strong financial background. Personal finance covers a range of topics, including budgeting, banking, insurance, mortgages, investments, retirement planning and tax and estate planning. Each of these topics could easily take a lifetime to understand fully.

To simplify personal finance, here are three basic rules to follow:

1. Save 10 to 20% of your salary every month without relying on credit card loans.

2. Invest your savings in a stock market index fund each month.

3. Purchase a term insurance plan to cover your dependents in case of your death.

These three rules encompass all of the significant aspects of personal finance, and they provide a starting point for saving and investing. Once you have a solid foundation, you can adjust the plan and incorporate more details as you become more knowledgeable about personal finance. These three rules cover savings, investing, tax planning, compounding, retirement, home loans, insurance and many other financial aspects.

This simple approach brings together complex concepts that work over time, including the savings habit from early career stages, compounding returns over the long term, tax efficiency with less trading within index funds for long-term capital gains, lower expenses with index funds, a single pool of money for emergencies or big purchases, 100% liquidity in case of emergencies and cheaper term insurance coverage in case of death.

Unfortunately, the financial industry may not appreciate this approach and may suggest different plans and schemes to collect fees for managing that complexity.

While many of us may have in-depth knowledge of our career professions, we may have limited knowledge of managing money. However, understanding and following basic money-management skills can give us control over our finances. It's crucial to master these skills, including budgeting, banking, saving, investing and understanding credit, to set ourselves up for future financial success.

1. Tracking expenses/creating a budget": Tracking expenses/creating a budget" involves ensuring that the balance in your chequebook register matches the balance in the monthly statement from your bank. To do so, you need to keep track of withdrawals and deposits and reconcile each entry in the register with the same transaction in your bank statement. The intention of this action is to know where your money is going every month and keep track of it. Whether you use a physical chequebook or an online one, you need to be in control of your account and the money that is being spent.

2. Setting up a budget: A budget is a plan for how to spend your money that factors in your income and expenses and it's the key to basic finance management of a household. If you don't know how much you can safely spend and save each month, you can easily go into debt or fail to meet long-term savings goals like retirement. Everyone should learn how to set up a realistic budget and plan to be successful later in life. Whether you use the envelope system,

where you separate all your cash for the month into separate envelopes, the zero-based budget that leaves no money at the end of the month, or a financial app, budgeting is a key money-management skill that everyone should master to live within their means.

3. Life Skills: Although these chores may not seem to relate to finances, grocery shopping, cooking, cleaning and other errands can save you a lot of money compared to dining out or using a meal-planning or maid service. With basic financial skills, you can find the best prices on food and fashion and plan practical menus to get you through college and beyond. Other skills like doing the laundry, mending clothes and performing simple car maintenance tasks on your own can help prolong the life of your possessions, ultimately saving you even more money. Eating home-packed lunches instead of dining out can save you a lot of money over the years.

4. Investing can be intimidating if you do not have at least a rudimentary understanding of how the stock market works and how to choose and invest in stocks. A basic investing class can

make a huge difference in how you handle your money. Learn basic investing principles in high school, such as asset allocation, diversification and rebalancing and you'll start your investing career ahead of the game. You can then jump-start your portfolio and retire earlier in life.

5. Long-Term Financial Planning: Understanding the need for a long-term plan for your money is a basic financial skill that you must master if you want to be financially secure in the future. Beyond learning how to budget, it involves learning how to set financial goals, prioritize them and develop a step-by-step plan for how to meet them. This process will lay the foundation for working towards major financial goals later in life, including paying off debts, saving for retirement, or buying your first home.

6. How to Build Credit and Manage Credit Cards: While many are targeted for credit card offers, chances are high that they lack the knowledge on how to use credit cards successfully. They often view them as extra money instead of looking at them as debt, spending money without having it. Of course, credit cards can be useful, but it depends on how you use them. They are the

downfall of many families. In addition to using credit cards, learning how to build credit and increase your credit score are basic financial skills. A good credit score can help you rent an apartment, qualify for lower interest rates on a mortgage or car loan, or even pay less for car insurance, so it's important to manage your credit history.

7. Renting vs. Buying a Home: In many cases, renting is cheaper than buying a house. However, many people are tempted to purchase a home, pay a high mortgage and decorate the property with the hope that its value will appreciate over time. But buying a home early in your career can limit your mobility and job options, forcing you to work for less just to stay in the same city. It's important to maintain flexibility in your living situation when starting out or when your children are young. This way, you can move around for better job opportunities and maximize your earnings potential. You can settle down and purchase a home later when you have more stability and can afford it.

DEBT Management

Avoiding debt or limiting loans is one of the most important parts of personal finance management. Debt can play both positive and negative roles in personal finance. Here are some ways debt can impact personal finances:

1. Positive role: Debt can help individuals achieve important goals that they may not be able to afford outright, such as buying a home, starting a business, or obtaining a college education. When used responsibly, debt can allow individuals to make investments in their future that can generate long-term financial benefits.

2. Negative role: Debt can also have a negative impact on personal finances if it is misused or becomes unmanageable. High levels of debt can lead to financial stress, make it difficult to qualify for credit in the future and cause damage to credit scores. Additionally, a high-interest debt, such as credit card debt, can accumulate quickly and become difficult to pay off.

3. Balancing debt: It's important to strike a balance between taking on debt for important goals and avoiding excessive levels of debt. This can involve

creating a budget and financial plan, minimizing high-interest debt and being mindful of the risks and costs associated with borrowing.

Here is an example of how debt can eat into your earnings over the long term:

Let's say you have a credit card with a balance of $5,000 and an annual interest rate of 18%. You make the minimum payment of $100 each month. Here is what your payment schedule and total interest paid would look like over time:

Month	Balance	Payment	Interest Paid	Total Interest Paid
1	$5,000	$100	$75.00	$75.00
2	$4,975	$100	$74.63	$149.63
3	$4,950	$100	$74.25	$223.88
...	...	...	...	...
24	$3,318	$100	$49.78	$1,403.38
25	$3,267	$100	$48.98	$1,452.36
...	...	...	...	...
36	$1,407	$100	$21.11	$2,423.31
37	$1,328	$100	$19.92	$2,443.23
...	...	...	...	...
48	$252	$100	$3.78	$2,947.09
49	$155	$100	$2.33	$2,974.42
50	$57	$57	$0.85	$2,975.27

As you can see, it would take over four years to pay off the credit card balance if you only make the minimum payment each month. And, over the long term, you would end up paying $2,975.27 in interest, which is almost as much as the original balance. This example illustrates how a high-interest debt can eat into your earnings over time and emphasizes the importance of paying off a debt as soon as possible to minimize its impact on your finances.

Financial IQ? CASH FLOW and TAXES (Salary vs. Capital Gains)

1. **Cash Flow:** Cash flow is a crucial factor in managing your personal finances. It refers to all the money coming in and going out of your pocket, regardless of your income level. Controlling your cash flow is essential to saving and investing money to build long-term wealth. Failure to manage cash flow can lead to accumulating liabilities such as credit card debts and personal loans. Once you have loans, it becomes increasingly difficult to improve cash flow, leading to a vicious cycle of interest payments, more loans and ultimately losing control of your finances.

It is vital to start saving at least 20% of your income in the early stages of your career to create assets that generate returns for the future. Assets, such as rental properties and stocks that appreciate in value or generate dividends, provide additional income without requiring your full-time engagement. Building assets is critical to achieving financial independence and long-term wealth. A person's financial IQ is determined by his or her ability to manage cash flow and create assets, regardless of income or education level.

2. **Taxes:** Understanding the tax system is the second most crucial aspect of achieving financial independence. The case of Warren Buffett's secretary, who pays more taxes than him despite earning far less, highlights the importance of understanding tax patterns.

Buffett's and many other billionaires' wealth comes mainly from capital gains on stock market investments, which are taxed much less than income tax in most countries. Income tax is deducted from salaries every month, while only capital gains tax is applied when you sell your stocks. This means that even though Buffett has a net worth of billions of dollars, he is not paying taxes on it until he sells some of his stocks. Money invested in the stock market continues to compound without any taxes for years or decades until it is sold, making it an advantageous option for building wealth compared to income from a salary.

Most countries' tax systems are designed to tax salaried individuals, who are the majority, while company owners and investors pay lower and delayed taxes. Therefore, it is essential to save and become an investor to build wealth, especially for salaried individuals.

Why Are These Skills Not Taught in High School or Degree?

In previous generations, students were often told to work hard, obtain an education, graduate and then enjoy the rewards of a well-paying job complete with pensions and other benefits. However, with the ever-changing world and technology, this is no longer as feasible as it once was. Unlike our fathers who worked for the same company for years, it is increasingly rare for our generation to have access to such job security and benefits. Some also suggest that there is a more sinister reason as to why financial literacy education is lacking: consumerism. When people take on more debt, they owe more money in interest payments to banks, corporations and others. Additionally, financial jargon can be complex and difficult for the average person to fully understand. This can have the effect of intimidating many adults and preventing them from asking critical questions about their financial well-being. We are simply taught that we need money to survive and put a roof over our heads. It can be easy for the average consumer to feel overwhelmed with financial information.

Many people make common financial mistakes that can lead to poor money management and loss of financial security. Here are some of the most common mistakes people make:

- As soon as we start our first job, we begin receiving our first pay cheque, and it can be an exciting time when we start living on our own money. However, we may end up making some common financial mistakes in the first few years of our careers, such as:

  o Saving money in savings accounts or fixed deposits, which is okay but not the best option for young career professionals.

  o Buying stocks without any knowledge or guidance, which is like gambling and can lead to inconsistent returns or even losses.

o   Investing in insurance policies recommended by our bank for investment purposes. Many of these policies have high expenses and low returns and it is better to handle insurance and investment decisions separately, with a term plan for insurance and investment decisions based solely on returns.

o   Falling into the vicious cycle of credit card debt by only paying the minimum balance. This can lead to high interest payments and a trap that is hard to get out of. It is always best to avoid having a balance on a credit card.

o   Changing our lifestyle for salary increments or bonuses. While yearly increments in salary or bonuses are good events to celebrate, they cannot be triggers for changing our lifestyle, such as moving from an apartment to a villa or upgrading a car, etc.

- Buying things just because they're on sale. It's important to consider whether you really need something before making a purchase, even if it's discounted. Companies often use sales to encourage people to buy unnecessary items, which can lead to financial waste.

- Getting tempted to go on an exotic vacation because of social media posts. Social media platforms like Facebook and Instagram can create envy and jealousy between friends. People often post content to gain likes and companies promote their products and services. It's important to remember that social media isn't real life and to consider your own financial situation before making travel plans.

- Having no idea where your money is going. It's crucial to track your expenses to understand your spending habits and adjust your budget accordingly. Most people don't keep a record of their expenses and may be surprised at how much they're spending.

- Not having an emergency budget. Unexpected expenses can happen at any time and it's important to have a financial cushion to fall back on. Borrowing money from friends or breaking investments can lead to further financial strain.

- Not having medical insurance. Healthcare costs are rising and one accident can lead to significant financial loss. It's important to have insurance to protect yourself and your finances.

- Not having a financial plan. Many people don't understand the importance of saving money and investing in their future. It's essential to set financial goals and create a plan to achieve them.

- Not diversifying investments. Putting all your money into one type of investment can be risky. It's important to diversify your investments to spread out risk and increase potential returns.

- Spending all your money on your children's weddings. In some cultures, it's common to spend a lot of money on weddings, which can deplete savings and leave little financial security for the future.

- Being extremely conservative with investments. Some people are risk-averse and avoid investing in anything other than low-risk options like fixed deposits. While these are safe investments, they may not offer the best returns. It's important to consider other investment options and find the right balance between risk and reward.

- Not understanding the difference between assets and liabilities. Assets are things that appreciate in value, while liabilities are things that cost money. A car, for example, is a liability because it requires maintenance and depreciates in value over time. It's important to understand the difference and make smart financial decisions.

- Confusing frugality with being cheap. Being frugal means being economical, not cheap. It's important to spend money wisely and not compromise on quality, even if you're looking for a good deal.

- Procrastinating investment decisions. Delaying investment decisions can lead to missed opportunities for compound earnings. It's important to make informed decisions and start investing as soon as possible.

- "Spending a lot of money on fancy stuff": People are willing to pay a premium for fancy cars, houses, watches and vacations, regardless of the value they generate.

- "Lack of patience": Many people want to double their investments in six months and blindly trust others with their money, leading to lifetime savings being lost. This happened to me in my 20s and helped me start a new journey with proper investments.

- "Depending on others for investment decisions": A lot of people depend on self-proclaimed experts for investment advice, resulting in the investment adviser making money irrespective of their returns. This is a losing strategy.

- "Getting too greedy with investment": People blindly invest in penny stocks, day trading, futures and options due to greed, resulting in losing everything they've earned.

- "Lack of disciplined investment": Instead of investing what's left after spending, people should spend what's left after investing. This results in disciplined investment and more money available for investing. It's better to take money out at the beginning of the month for investment and live within the means of what's left over after investing.

- "No diversification": Very few people understand the right way to diversify their investments. Some invest all their money in real estate, gold, or the stock market, while others keep it in the locker.

- "An extremely conservative approach with investment": Traditionally, people have been risk-averse, living on 6-7% annual interest from FDs or keeping cash at home. I know many smart professionals making good money but not putting it to work with proper investments.

- "Lack of clarity between asset and liability": A car is not an asset because it consumes fuel and has a maintenance cost. Its price will only depreciate in the future. People spend a lot of money and even take a loan to buy a luxury car above their budget. Assets grow in value over time and give returns like rental units of apartments or shops.

- "Considering frugal as cheap": Economic spending is not the same as being cheap. Economic spenders do not compromise on quality but research well to buy products or services at the lowest rate. It's essential to ensure the need for a product or service before buying it just because it's on sale.

In summary, you can take control of your finances and build a secure financial future by avoiding these mistakes. **One simple principle for personal finance is to earn before you spend and understand the basics of investing.**

"Yes… Money doesn't solve ALL problems, but it could solve many money problems."

Part II: MANTRA for Wealth Creation (3 SEC MANTRA) – Savings, Emotional Intelligence and Compounding

Chapter 5: Savings – Consistent Saving and Investing

Saving and investing every month is one of the most important financial habits that one can cultivate. It not only helps individuals meet their financial goals but also ensures long-term financial stability. In this essay, we will discuss the importance of saving and investing every month and the benefits it offers.

Firstly, saving and investing every month help individuals build a financial safety net. It ensures that they have enough funds to cover unforeseen expenses, emergencies, or any other unexpected financial need. It also helps them avoid borrowing money or taking out loans, which can lead to high interest rates and debt. Additionally, having a financial safety net can reduce stress and provide peace of mind, knowing that they are prepared for any financial setback.

Secondly, saving and investing every month help individuals achieve their financial goals. Whether it's buying a house, saving for a child's education, or planning for retirement, regular savings and investments can help them reach these goals more quickly. By consistently putting money away, they can take advantage of the power of compounding, which can significantly increase their savings over time. This can lead to a more comfortable lifestyle, financial security and the ability to achieve their dreams.

Thirdly, saving and investing every month can help individuals become financially independent. By regularly saving and investing, they can create a stream of passive income that can support them in their retirement years. This can provide them with the freedom to pursue their interests, travel, or spend time with family without having to worry about financial constraints.

Lastly, saving and investing every month help individuals develop discipline and financial responsibility. By making it a habit to save and invest, they can learn to live within their means and avoid overspending. They can also learn to prioritize their financial goals and make informed decisions about their money.

In conclusion, saving and investing every month is an essential financial habit that can provide individuals with numerous benefits. It can help them build a financial safety net, achieve their financial goals, become financially independent and develop financial responsibility. By making it a priority to save and invest regularly, they can improve their financial well-being and enjoy a more secure future.

As a working professional, it is important to have the right skills that are in demand in the market. These skills will help you secure the right job or contract or customers and make good money. While this is an important foundation for living a good life, saving a percentage of this money consistently is equally important for future lifestyle and achieving financial freedom. These savings are necessary during the initial years to gain freedom from a pay cheque and pursue your passion without worrying about salary or starting a business.

The next question after deciding to save is how much and in which phase of life. This decision depends on your comfort and commitment and can range from 10% to 40% of your gross income, depending on your expenses and phase of life. It's best to save more in the early part of your career as these savings have the longest time to work for you until retirement. One commitment you must make is to never dip into these savings. Start with 20% and adjust the percentage higher or lower depending on your comfort after a couple of months.

Here's how you can do it. Every month, a portion of your salary is deducted as income tax without you seeing or touching that money. For example, if your gross salary is 12L per annum and 10% is income tax on average, you will get around 90K per month, with 10K deducted towards tax. Plan your monthly expenses around 90K only and never think of the 10K going to the government. Similarly, if you decide to save 20% of your take-home pay, you will have to plan monthly expenses around 72K (90K – 18K) per month. The remaining 18K will go into an indexing SIP automatically every month. Set up a recurring SIP that will automatically deduct this money from your salary account and invest it in a stock market index like SENSEX.

Chapter Summary/Key Takeaways: The chapter discusses the importance of saving and investing every month, highlighting the benefits it offers, such as building a financial safety net, achieving financial goals, becoming financially independent and developing discipline and financial responsibility. The author emphasizes that consistent saving is essential for future lifestyle and financial freedom. The suggested amount to save ranges from 10% to 40% of gross income, depending on expenses and life phase, with a recommendation to start with 20%

and adjust accordingly. The author suggests setting up a recurring SIP to automatically deduct the saved amount from the salary account and invest it in a stock market index. Overall, the chapter encourages individuals to prioritize saving and investing to improve their financial well-being and secure a more secure future.

Chapter 6:
Emotional Intelligence – Ride Out Market Swings and Market Timing Temptations

The stock market is a complex and volatile environment where investing decisions are often driven by emotions. However, it is essential to understand that emotions should not be the factor driving investment decisions. This is where emotional intelligence comes into play. Emotional intelligence is a critical skill that can help investors make better decisions, especially when it comes to the stock market. Emotional stability plays a crucial role in stock market investment and wealth-building over the long term. As Warren Buffett famously said, "If you have a 150 IQ, sell 30 points to someone else. You need to be smart, but not a genius." He emphasizes the importance of rationality and emotional stability in investing.

Emotional intelligence (EQ) is particularly valuable in stock market indexing because it can help investors manage their emotions and make rational investment decisions. EQ involves recognizing, understanding and managing one's own emotions as well as those of others. In investing, EQ can help investors avoid making impulsive decisions based on fear or greed and instead make thoughtful, strategic decisions based on market trends and analysis. Investing in the stock market requires discipline, patience and the ability to stay focused on long-term goals. Emotional intelligence helps investors develop these qualities and avoid common pitfalls, such as buying or selling stocks based on short-term market trends or headlines.

For example, consider the case of a company whose stock price falls suddenly due to negative news. A person without emotional intelligence may panic and sell their shares, fearing that the stock will continue to fall. However, a person with emotional intelligence may take a step back and evaluate the situation more objectively, considering the company's overall financial health, long-term prospects and the potential impact of the news on its future performance. This person is less likely to make impulsive decisions and more likely to stay committed to their investment strategy.

Indexing is a passive investment strategy in which investors simply buy and hold a diversified portfolio of stocks that mirrors a particular index, such as the S&P 500. This approach helps investors avoid emotional decision-making, as they are not actively buying and selling individual stocks based on market fluctuations.

However, emotions can still come into play even with an index fund, particularly during times of market volatility. For example, during a market downturn, investors may feel panicked and want to sell their shares, even if the index fund they are invested in has a long-term track record of strong performance. In these situations, having high emotional intelligence can help investors stay calm and focused, enabling them to stick to their long-term investment strategy and ride out the temporary market fluctuations.

In summary, emotional intelligence is an essential factor in successful stock market indexing, helping investors make rational decisions, avoid impulsive behaviours, and stay focused on their long-term investment goals. In conclusion, emotional intelligence is an essential skill for successful stock market investing. It allows investors to manage their own emotions and make rational, long-term investment decisions. Additionally, it helps them understand better and empathize with the motivations of other market participants, allowing for more informed and strategic investment decisions. By incorporating emotional intelligence into their investment strategies, investors can improve their chances of achieving their financial goals and navigate the complex and ever-changing world of the stock market. Typical mistakes made while investing are often due to a lack of emotional intelligence. Here are a few examples:

1. Lack of understanding of the investment: We may make investments based on a recommendation from a friend or media news without conviction or reason. In such scenarios, when that investment starts going down, we may panic and probably sell at the wrong time when it's really low. It's important to understand the company/investment and the rationale for the investment. It's okay to make a mistake in this rationale and realize that our decision is wrong and sell it, but not just with emotion when it starts going down.

2. Bias or attachment towards an investment or company: We all have biases towards people and investments. The goal is to reduce attachment or bias towards our investment or company. When we have bias or attachment towards a company,

we may not be able to see the negative business trend of the company. For example, I love my iPhone as a consumer, but evaluating Apple stock for investment is a completely different process. My love for the iPhone should not impact my decision to buy/sell Apple stock. It's just a single user feedback and can't be the whole criteria for buying stock.

3. Impatience and too many purchases/sales of investment: It's similar to the first point on conviction of the investment. When we don't have that conviction, we end up getting impatient and making more trades with our money.

4. Trying to time the market or chase market momentum: Buffett said, "Market timing is a loser's game." We may get lucky a few times, but in the end, we end up on the losing side.

5. Letting our emotions decide or lack of rationale for decisions: We need to be rational with our decisions with proper logic and conviction. Emotions can't rule our investing decisions. Most decisions made in high emotion, like anger or sadness, are usually wrong judgements.

Slow-paced Investing in the Fast-paced World

We are living in a fast-paced world where everything happens spontaneously. It is an instant gratification world and as a society, we are becoming increasingly impatient. We want things to happen instantly, whether it's an Uber ride, an Amazon delivery, or a Swiggy food delivery, all with the click of a button and within a matter of hours or a day at the most. In the technology world, IT professionals are trained and rewarded for delivering Agile projects, which means delivering value to customers quickly in increments in long projects.

In today's fast-paced world, people are often seeking quick solutions, immediate gratification and instant results. This is particularly true when it comes to investing in the stock market, where many individuals are lured by the promises of quick profits and rapid returns. However, it is essential to recognize that successful investing requires **patience, discipline, and a long-term perspective**. This is where slow-paced index investing comes in – a strategy that emphasizes the value of patience and consistency.

Index investing involves buying and holding a diversified portfolio of stocks that mimic the performance of a particular market index, such as the S&P 500 or the

Dow Jones Industrial Average. Unlike actively managed funds that attempt to beat the market by choosing individual stocks or timing the market, index funds simply track the performance of the underlying index. This approach has gained popularity in recent years, as research has shown that index investing typically outperforms actively managed funds over the long term.

However, the success of index investing hinges on the ability of investors to remain patient and disciplined in the face of short-term market volatility. This is where emotional intelligence comes into play – the ability to recognize and manage emotions in oneself and others. Emotional intelligence is particularly important in the context of investing because it helps individuals make rational decisions based on long-term goals, rather than short-term market fluctuations.

Similarly, relationships, fitness, social impact and leadership all require a long-term commitment. It's like brushing your teeth every morning and night before you go to bed. You need to do it consistently every day to keep your teeth healthy. This principle also applies to areas where we want to feel the impact created by our work. The millennial generation needs to understand and experience this for a good life. In the startup world, you can fail fast and move quickly to improve your business plan, but building relationships with people and wealth requires long-term planning and commitment.

Chapter Summary/Key Takeaways: The chapter discussed the importance of emotional intelligence in successful stock market investing, especially in the context of ndexing. Emotional intelligence helps investors make rational decisions, avoid impulsive behaviours and stay focused on their long-term investment goals. Emotional intelligence involves recognizing, understanding and managing one's own emotions, as well as those of others. Indexing is a passive investment strategy that helps investors avoid emotional decision-making. However, emotions can still come into play during market volatility and high emotional intelligence can help investors stay calm and focused. The chapter also highlights common mistakes made while investing, such as a lack of understanding of the investment, bias or attachment towards an investment, impatience, trying to time the market and letting emotions decide investment decisions. The chapter concludes by emphasizing the need for rational decisions with proper logic and conviction in a fast-paced world where people often seek quick solutions and immediate gratification.

Chapter 7: Compounding: Eighth Wonder of the World!

Let me start with a story of a chess game between a king and a sage. The king, who had a deep interest in chess, played the game with the sage, offering to give him anything he wanted if he lost, including diamonds. The sage had a simple request – to give him rice in the following manner: a single grain of rice on the first chess square, 2 grains in the second chess square, 4 grains in the third chess square and similarly double it on every consequent square. The king accepted the sage's request. However, the king soon realized the magnitude of the task and could not meet the sage's request. By the 20th square, the king would have had to put 1,000,000 grains of rice. On the 40th square, he would have had to put 1,000,000,000 grains of rice. Finally, on the 64th square, the king would have had to put more than 18,000,000,000,000,000,000 grains of rice, which is equal to about 210 billion tonnes and would allegedly be sufficient to cover the whole territory of India with a metre-thick layer of rice. This story exemplifies the power of compounding and you want this compounding to work for you with your savings over life.

Compounding is the process of earning interest on your principal investment and then earning interest on the interest that has accumulated over time. This means that your investment can grow at an exponential rate, even if you don't add any additional funds. For example, if you invest $10,000 and earn a 10% annual return, you will have $11,000 at the end of the first year. If you earn another 10% return on that $11,000 in the second year, you will have $12,100 at the end of the second year. Over time, the amount of interest earned on the interest earned becomes increasingly significant and your investment can grow to significant amounts.

The key to taking advantage of compounding is to start investing as early as possible and to be consistent with your contributions. The longer your money is invested, the more time it has to compound and grow. This is why it's important to start saving for retirement as soon as you can, even if it's just a small amount each month.

Compounding is also why it's important to avoid high fees and expenses when investing. Fees and expenses can eat away at your returns, reducing the amount of money available to compound. This is why index funds, which have lower fees than actively managed funds, can be a good choice for investors who want to take advantage of compounding. By keeping expenses low, you can maximize the power of compounding and grow your wealth over time. Compounding is a powerful concept in investing, often referred to as the "eighth wonder of the world" by some of the most successful investors in history. At its core, compounding is the ability to earn interest on interest. Over time, this simple concept can lead to incredible wealth creation. **The time horizon for investing is one of the most important elements for wealth creation**. When you are just starting out in your career, it gives you flexibility with fewer expenses as a single person and these savings will work best for you due to the long-time horizon. Understanding this and acting during this early phase of life will do wonders for the later part of life. Many of us will miss this opportunity during the early part of our careers for various reasons:

1. We do not understand the value of investing early.

2. Most of us will not have enough knowledge of investing.

3. Even if you want to invest, you do not know where to start.

4. The trading industry, banks and media will confuse us so much that we mostly either postpone the investment or get into stock trading.

Let's look at an example below to highlight the magic of compounding with the difference between saving early vs. late.

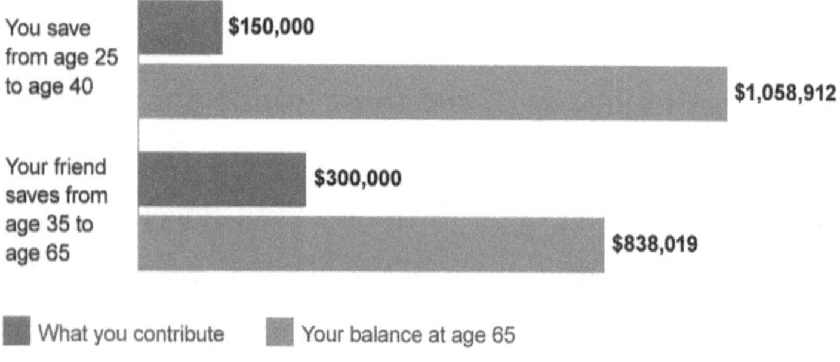

It's not just the size of your initial investment that matters. The length of time your investment has to compound is equally or more important. Consider the following scenario: You invest $10,000 every year from 25 to 40. By the time you reach age 65, your investment would be worth over $1058912. However, if you waited until age 35 to start investing for the same $10,000 investment and continue till 65, it would only be worth around $838019 by the time of age 65. Though the invested amount is double in the second scenario, the final amount at 65 is higher in scenario-1 due to starting early. This example highlights the importance of starting early and allowing your investments time to compound. **Though your contribution amount is only half of what you do in the second scenario, your amount at retirement age is 20% more than in the second scenario.**

One of the powerful tools for compounding in investing is the reinvestment of dividends. Dividends are payments made by companies to shareholders as a yield for owning their stock. When dividends are reinvested, they can grow exponentially over time. For example, imagine you own 100 shares of a company that pays a $1 dividend each year. If you reinvest those dividends and earn an average annual return of 10%, your investment would be worth over $1,500 after 10 years. However, if you chose to take the dividends as cash, your investment would only be worth $1,000 after 10 years. By reinvesting dividends, you are allowing your investment to compound even more rapidly.

It's important to note that while compounding can be incredibly powerful, it is not a guarantee. There is always some level of risk involved in investing and returns can fluctuate over time. Additionally, fees and expenses can eat into your returns, reducing the amount of money available to compound. This is why it's important to choose low-cost investments, such as index funds and to diversify your portfolio to reduce risk.

In conclusion, compounding is a powerful concept in investing that can lead to incredible wealth creation over time. By starting early, reinvesting dividends and choosing low-cost investments, you can maximize the power of compounding and grow your wealth for the long term.

Appreciating the power of compounding takes time and it is called the eighth wonder of the world for the same reason. Can you imagine this? Starting with Rs.10000 per month savings at 21 years can make you a millionaire at 50 years.

Chapter Summary/Key Takeaways: This chapter discussed the importance of compounding for building wealth and why it is called the eighth wonder of the world. It also highlighted the example of savings less early in life can result in a higher amount at age 65 compared to double savings at the latter part of life. We can now bring together the 3-SEC mantra to make a million dollars (8+ crores of Indian rupees) with just Rs. 10000 savings per month.

Chapter 8:
How to Become a
$ Millionaire With
Rs. 10,000 Per Month
Savings?

Do you think being a dollar millionaire is out of the question for you? Think again. Even those with meagre earnings can become a millionaire if **they're diligent with savings, manage their investments and stick with it for long enough**. Here are some examples of how you can become a dollar millionaire through steady saving habits. Stock market indexing is the easiest way to become a millionaire over a long period of time.

Becoming a millionaire is a dream for many people, but it can seem like an impossible goal to achieve. However, with smart saving and investing strategies, it is possible to make this dream a reality. If you are willing to save and invest consistently, even a small amount of money can grow significantly over time due to the power of compounding. Here's how you can become a millionaire with savings of Rs. 10,000 per month:

1. Start early: Time is the most important factor when it comes to investing. The earlier you start, the more time your money has to grow. Even if you are in your 20s, it's never too late to start investing. The power of compounding means that even small investments can grow significantly over time.

2. Invest in index funds: Index funds are a great way to invest in the stock market without having to pick individual stocks. These funds track the performance of a market index, such as the Nifty 50 or the BSE SENSEX and provide broad market exposure at a low cost. By investing in index funds, you can benefit from the long-term growth of the stock market while keeping your fees and expenses low.

3. Increase your savings rate: While Rs. 10,000 per month is a great start, if you want to become a millionaire faster, you need to increase your savings rate. Look for ways to cut back on expenses and increase your income so that you can save more money each month.

4. Avoid debt: Debt can be a major hindrance to wealth accumulation. If you have high-interest debt, such as credit card debt or personal loans, prioritize paying it off before you start investing. This will allow you to put more money towards your investments in the long run.

5. Reinvest your dividends: If you are investing in stocks or mutual funds that pay dividends, reinvest them instead of taking them as cash. Reinvesting your dividends allows you to take advantage of the power of compounding and can significantly increase your returns over time.

6. Be patient: Building wealth takes time and patience. Don't get discouraged if your investments don't show significant returns in the short term. Focus on your long-term goals and stay committed to your savings and investing plan.

By following these tips and staying disciplined with your savings and investing, it is possible to become a millionaire with just Rs. 10,000 per month as savings. The key is to start early, invest in low-cost index funds, increase your savings rate, avoid debt, reinvest your dividends and be patient. With time and dedication, you can achieve your financial goals and secure your financial future.

Primary Factors Affecting Millionaire Status

Becoming a millionaire is an achievable goal, but it requires careful attention to two critical factors: debt and time. If you can avoid consumer debt and begin investing in your 20s or 30s, you can achieve millionaire status by the time you retire. While it may take time to build up your initial investment, you will be surprised at how quickly your savings can grow thanks to the power of compounding.

Let's consider an example of how someone starting with Rs. 10,000 in savings per month at age 21 can achieve millionaire status. Even if your net monthly income is Rs. 50,000, saving 20% of it is a reasonable goal. Of course, if you earn more than Rs. 50,000, you can reach the millionaire status even more quickly and easily.

Assuming a 10% annual increase in savings in line with income growth and a standard 15% annual return on investment, let's see how your savings can multiply over time. We'll also assume that you make a one-time expense of a car with a Rs. 2 lakh down payment at age

24 and a home with a Rs. 10 lakh down payment at age 29, both paid from your savings.

Age	Amount
21	1.2L
27	15L
33	50L
36	1.0 cr
41	2.4 cr
46	5.65 cr
48	7.8 cr ($ Millionaire)

Please look at the way the amount grows very slowly at the beginning as the amount was only 15L after the first six years but it went to 50L in the next six years and 1.0 cr in the following three years. Money starts working for you to create more money with time. What it means is the sooner you start this money-making machine at the beginning of your life, the better it works for you for the rest of your life.

Three important things are at work for this magic to work:

1. Start early with small amounts and continue the discipline to save.

2. Due to indexing, expenses and taxes are most efficient leaving more money with you.

3. Compounding effect and safety are on your side due to the long-term horizon.

Chapter Summary/Key Takeaways: To summarize, anyone can become a millionaire or *crorepati* if they can save some money every month. It requires strong discipline to save every month, commitment to indexing and understanding the magic of compounding with taxation working for you. Example here is just a case in point and you can do either Rs. 5000 a month or Rs. 20000 a month based on your financial situation and salary and your amount at the end of your age will be half and double the amounts in that table. The most important point is to SAVE SOME MONEY AT AN EARLY AGE. AMOUNT MATTERS LESS as it depends on your individual salary and financial situation. There is never a better time than to START NOW. We need to understand the value of compounding and follow at least 80% of the above process with 20% exceptional scenarios like losing a job or other crises which may impact the plan above.

Part III: Stock Market Investing

There are several ways to invest in the stock market:

1. Individual Stocks: You can invest in individual stocks by buying shares of a specific company that is publicly traded on a stock exchange.

2. Mutual Funds: Mutual funds are a collection of stocks that are managed by a professional fund manager. You can invest in mutual funds by buying shares of the fund which gives you exposure to a diversified portfolio of stocks.

3. Exchange-Traded Funds (ETFs): ETFs are similar to mutual funds, but they trade like individual stocks. ETFs allow you to invest in a diversified portfolio of stocks that track an index, such as the S&P 500.

4. Index funds: Index funds are a type of mutual fund or ETF that tracks a specific stock market index, such as the Dow Jones Industrial Average or the NASDAQ Composite.

5. Options: Options are a type of derivative that allows you to buy or sell a stock at a specific price in the future.

6. Futures: Futures are similar to options in that they allow you to buy or sell a stock at a specific

price in the future, but they are standardized contracts that trade on exchanges.

7. Margin Trading: Margin trading allows you to borrow money from a broker to invest in stocks. This can increase your potential gains, but it also increases your potential losses.

It is important to note that investing in the stock market involves risk, and it is important to do your research and understand the potential risks before investing. It is also recommended to consult with a financial adviser before making any investment decisions.

We will talk about three major ways to participate in the market: Stock picking, mutual funds and indexing. There are many different variations of these like options, futures, day trading, etc. but we will keep them out of this conversation as they are more like casino gambling than real investing. General opinion and mistrust of the stock market come from these where you can lose or gain money out of thin air without any fundamentals at stake.

Chapter 9:
Stock Market Investing Methods

Stock Picking

Picking individual stocks for investing in the stock market is a profession in itself. It requires a deep understanding of business fundamentals, balance sheets, income statements, market potential and more. Each of these topics requires detailed study and expertise. Company valuation and security analysis are areas in which one can obtain a degree to master this profession. "The Intelligent Investor" by Benjamin Graham is the bible for security analysis and picking individual stocks based on fundamentals. Anyone can learn it, but it is a profession that requires deep knowledge and effort, like any other profession.

For those in professions such as IT, Law, or Medicine, getting into stock picking is similar to an engineer going into an operating room and attempting to perform a surgery. It's not something that people would allow as it poses a risk to others/patients. In the stock market, the risk is to your own money and that's why everyone has the freedom to pick stocks because you are taking a risk with your own money. However, we need to understand the dangerous nature of this practice. This is not to say that it's impossible, but we need to understand the complexity and effort required to do a good job.

There are some exceptional individuals who do this full-time and do well over the long run. There are also teams and companies working on picking stocks. Here is what they typically have at their disposal:

- A team of professionals with a degree in Security Analysis

- Years of experience and learnings from doing this job

- Company resources and support for additional research material on a company

- Relationships with executives to get insight into a company

- 8+ hours a day of time at their disposal

When we are into stock picking or trading, we are trying to do this while working a full-time job under many constraints like limited time, no professional degree or knowledge and no access to the leadership team. How can we do a better job of picking the right stocks compared to these professionals? Sometimes, it works like a lottery or gut feeling, but many times we end up on the wrong side. Doing this is similar to flipping a coin, and sometimes you win just by luck.

Without properly understanding how we are stacked against a wall, we jump into the stock market either due to pressure from a marketing trading company or stories from our friends on how they made easy money in the stock market. We need to understand that our friends will not share their failure stories and they only highlight their success stories.

This is like playing cricket against Virat Kohli & India team and trying to win the game. We know it's impossible, but we still try to do it in the stock market, hoping against all odds. Many people do it because it gives them that adrenaline rush or the experience of a rollercoaster ride of WIN or LOSE instantly. It's good with small money in the short term just for the experience, but you don't want to do this with your long-term wealth and a significant part of your money.

Very few people have mastered this art and they have made millions of dollars in the stock market. If you have truly mastered this, it's time to quit your full-time job and spend your time doing this to make much more money than just limiting yourself to simple stock picking for yourself. Warren Buffett, in the early part of his life, mastered this and made billions of dollars for his family and friends by investing their money and he made a lot of money along the way.

Mutual Funds

We discussed how challenging it is to consistently pick individual stocks and be successful over 40+ years of a professional career. One solution to this problem is investing in mutual funds. A Mutual Fund is managed by a professional with a degree in stock market investing. It is usually a collection of multiple company stocks or bonds and its value goes up or down based on the performance of the stocks and bonds within the fund. The fund will have a dedicated manager who actively manages the portfolio and trades stocks based on their knowledge and market research. This is a good option compared to picking individual stocks, as you are relying on a professional to do the work for you. However, there are additional costs associated with managing the fund, which are distributed among those investing in the mutual fund. The company that owns the mutual fund, such as HDFC or ICICI, will also look to make money by running the fund.

In 2008, Warren Buffett issued a challenge to the fund industry, claiming that they charged exorbitant fees that the funds' performances couldn't justify. Protégé Partners LLC accepted the challenge and the two parties placed a million-dollar bet. Buffett won the bet, as Protégé co-founder Ted Seides wrote in a Bloomberg op-ed in May. Seides conceded defeat ahead of the contest's scheduled wrap-up on December 31, 2017, writing, "For all intents and purposes, the game is over. I lost."

As you can see, there are also challenges with mutual funds, as you are trusting one fund manager to decide on stocks to buy or sell. Another issue is too many trades and taxes on all those trades. In US history, there was not a single mutual fund that consistently delivered better returns than the average stock market returns. Some fund managers did it for 10 to 15 years. That brings us to the third option, which is indexing.

When stock markets go up, human behaviour of greed takes over and the market and stocks become very irrational. We need to understand that stock price is just a reflection of the business of the company. Investors can make money in the stock market in three ways: dividends from the stock (profit of the company), growth of the business and lower or higher valuation based on daily sentiment. The first two elements are grounded in the business fundamentals of the company, while the third element is just a mood or sentiment of the crowd on that day or time. It can change any day and this is what we witness in markets going up crazily or crashing crazily in a short duration.

When people talk about stock market investing using trading, they are essentially going into the third category. Yes, many do some basic checking, follow industry pundits' stock predictions, stock tip secrets, etc., but mostly it is based on sentiment. It works if the markets are going up and you feel very smart and intelligent. This goes on for years sometimes, as it happened from the 1990s to 2000 and recently from 2008 to 2021. Much of this is also tied to sunrise industries like the Internet and Tech companies. We experienced a great Tech bubble burst in 2000 and now something similar is happening in 2023 with many Tech companies crashing to 20% of their valuations like SHOP, HOOD, TWLO, etc.

This continuous cycle of the stock market going up and down makes us feel like there is an opportunity to make a lot of money. After the fact, we hear stories of someone who bought great companies at an early stage and would be a millionaire by now. But the fact is, there is no way for anyone to know ahead of time. Even experts like Warren Buffett have missed out on investing in many great companies at an early stage. The secret to successful investing is not about finding the next Microsoft or Apple, but rather betting on the economies of countries that are likely to perform well in the long run based on their political systems, current size and future expectations. For instance, it is easier to predict that a country like India will continue to grow over the next 20 to 30 years than to say that a particular company like Zomato or Swiggy will perform well over the same period.

Stock Market Indexing

The stock market index is chosen by a group of professionals who select the stocks that represent the index. For instance, BSE SENSEX consists of 30 stocks that are picked by experts and changes to the index are reviewed infrequently. Stock market indexing is a passive investment style that doesn't require active research or trading. It involves investing blindly in stocks that represent the index.

Most mutual fund companies offer index mutual funds that track or mimic various indexes. These index funds are low in expenses because they don't have to spend money and time on researching companies. Instead, they invest blindly in the same stocks that represent the index. They also have lower trading charges and taxes as most of the returns are long-term. Although this investment style may not seem exciting or interesting in the short term, over a 40+ year investment period, it can work wonders for several reasons, such as the power of compounding, consistent performance based on the intelligence of experts, lower expenses and taxes. Since its inception in 1979, SENSEX has given a compounded annual growth rate of 17% p.a., which is a huge return over a long period of time.

Stock Market Timing – Buy Low and Sell High 😊

This is another misconception that stems from human psychology where we strongly feel that we can time the market. It is challenging to accept this truth even after multiple failures to time the market. You may have examples of stocks bought at the wrong time or sold too early. Personally, I have been doing stock market indexing for the last 20 years and although I am strongly committed to the overall concept, I have made the mistake of trying to time the market. I learned the hard way that you need to get this right twice. I sold when the index was at a high of SENSEX 36000 and it went down to around 24000. I felt good about escaping the fall, but it started going up again and I never got the right time to enter the market, expecting it to fall again. I ended up entering the market again when the index was around 44000, which means effectively, I lost the gains from 36000 to 44000, even though I got one of the two timing decisions correct. Then I realized what Buffett meant when he said, "Market timing is a loser's game ☺."

Chapter Summary/Key Takeaways: To summarize, stock picking requires a lot of knowledge, time and effort. It is extremely challenging for a full-time career professional to pick individual stocks and be successful in the long run. Mutual funds are a decent option but it has an added layer of expenses and taxes with dependency on a single fund manager. The best option is **stock market indexing**. Indexing leverages the expertise of groups of professionals and at the same time avoids the majority of expenses of mutual funds with lower taxes.

In the next chapter, you will learn more about indexing fundamentals and what makes it the best option for a career professional.

Chapter 10: Stock Market Indexing

History of Index Mutual Funds

"The Intelligent Investor" book is considered the bible for stock market investing as it teaches how to analyse stocks based on their fundamentals to evaluate the value of a company and compare it to the stock price for buying or selling decisions. The book was written by Benjamin Graham, a professor at Columbia University and is regarded as the father of value investing. Warren Buffett considers Graham his guru and credits his success to this book, strongly recommending it to anyone getting into stock picking for investing.

Although mutual funds existed for a long time, they gained popularity in the 1980s due to a bull market in the US and as a good retirement option in 401K retirement accounts. John Bogle introduced the first index fund for tracking the US S&P 500 index and founded the Vanguard Mutual Fund company, which is the largest publicly traded mutual fund company in the US and mainly focuses on index funds.

Stock market indexing is a popular investment strategy that involves investing in a diverse portfolio of stocks that track a particular market index, such as the S&P 500 or the NASDAQ. The aim of this strategy is to replicate the performance of the underlying index, providing investors with a low-cost way to gain exposure to the broad stock market.

The fundamentals of stock market indexing are based on the efficient market hypothesis, which suggests that it is impossible to consistently beat the market over the long term. Instead of trying to outperform the market, index fund investors seek to match the performance of the market by investing in a representative sample of stocks.

One of the key advantages of stock market indexing is that it offers investors diversification, which is the process of spreading their investments across a range of different assets to reduce risk. By investing in an index fund, investors gain exposure to many stocks, thereby spreading their risk across multiple companies and sectors.

Another advantage of stock market indexing is that it typically involves lower fees and expenses than actively managed funds. Because index funds do not require the same level of research and analysis as actively managed funds, they are often less expensive to operate. This means that investors can benefit from lower costs and fees, which can have a significant impact on long-term returns.

Finally, stock market indexing is a simple and straightforward investment strategy that requires little knowledge or expertise. With index funds, investors do not need to worry about choosing individual stocks or timing the market, which can be difficult and time-consuming. Instead, investors can simply buy and hold an index fund, enjoying the long-term benefits of stock market growth and compounding returns.

Stress-free With Limited Knowledge Requirement

The best thing about stock indexing is that it requires limited or zero knowledge of stocks and is completely stress-free. You will not have to worry about daily stock market swings, as you know that your long-term investment is 100% protected. Ideally, you should not check or look at the stock market at all. Day trades go through so many emotional swings as the market or stocks go up and down, taking time away from work and family life.

Diversification

Diversification is the foundation of any stock market investing portfolio. Warren Buffett summarized this in his simple quote: "Don't put all your eggs in one basket." The stock market is a risky investment asset, so it is super important to create a diverse portfolio to protect your principal. Diversification here is very broad and can mean, at the lowest level, investing in multiple stocks of different industries, to stocks, bonds and cash, to investing in multiple countries. Depending on the size of the portfolio, you need to decide on the right diversification.

When you pick an index, it automatically provides diversification. If you have Rs. 10,000 and invest in an index fund like SENSEX 30, effectively you bought 30 company stocks that represent the BSE SENSEX index in one shot.

Systematic Investment Plan (SIP)

Systematic Investment Plans (SIPs) are a method of investing in mutual funds that allows investors to make small, periodic investments over a longer period of time. It is a disciplined approach to investment that encourages regular savings and helps investors achieve their financial goals.

All index funds support SIP and strongly encourage it without any additional charges. This is also known as DCA (Dollar Cost Averaging) in the US. It helps us avoid entering the market with a full amount at the peak and helps us average out the buying price over the long run. When the price is lower, or the market is down, we buy more units for the same cost and it really helps increase our return when the market bounces back.

As full-time career professionals, our income streams are constant and fixed over a year. We can leverage this as an asset with continuous fixed amount automatic investment. Indexing along with SIP is the lethal combination to make money in the stock market over the long term. A simple strategy to employ is to get started with an index investment with a small amount like Rs. 10,000, with an SIP of Rs. 2,000 per month and continue to increase it based on your comfort and confidence.

Here are some advantages of investing through SIPs in index funds:

Disciplined investment approach: SIPs help investors invest regularly, which in turn helps to accumulate wealth over a longer period of time. This disciplined approach reduces the risk of investing a lump sum amount in one go and also helps to overcome the impact of market volatility.

Averaging out of cost: Since SIPs allow investors to invest a fixed amount at regular intervals, it helps to average out the cost of investments. This means that investors can buy more units when the market is low and fewer units when the market is high, resulting in a lower average cost of investment. This helps investors buy more units when the market is low and fewer units when the market is high, thereby reducing the impact of market volatility on their investments.

Flexibility is one of the key advantages of SIPs in index funds. Investors have the option to choose the amount they want to invest and the frequency of investment based on their financial goals and investment objectives. This allows investors to create a customized investment plan that is tailored to their specific needs. For instance, an investor who is looking to save for a long-term financial goal may choose to invest a larger amount in SIPs on a monthly or quarterly basis.

Another advantage of SIPs in index funds is the low minimum investment amount. Many mutual fund companies offer SIPs with a low minimum investment amount, making them accessible to a wider range of investors. This is particularly beneficial for first-time investors who may not have a large amount of capital to invest. Investing in SIPs with a low minimum investment amount can help investors start their investment journey and gradually increase their investment over time.

Furthermore, investing in SIPs in index funds can help investors overcome the impact of market volatility. Index funds are diversified investments that track the performance of a market index, such as the S&P 500. This means that the performance of the fund is not tied to the performance of any individual stock. As a result, index funds tend to be less volatile than individual stocks, which can help investors avoid the impact of sudden market fluctuations.

In conclusion, investing in SIPs in index funds is a great way to start investing in the stock market. They are low-cost, flexible and can help investors overcome the impact of market volatility. It is important to conduct thorough research and choose the right index fund that matches your investment goals and risk profile. With the right approach, investing in SIPs in index funds can be a smart and effective way to build wealth over the long term.

Bouncing Back from Market Downturns

Although the SENSEX experiences downturns from time to time, it has always bounced back in the long run. While there have been instances where the SENSEX has crashed by 20% or even 50% in the short term, it has always bounced back over the long term, and now it stands at around 50,000. However, this is not necessarily true for individual companies. Over the years, many companies have gone completely out of business. Companies that are part of the SENSEX 30 index are evaluated based on their business health and potential. They are removed and new companies are added based on this evaluation. With this adjustment, the index will continue to go up almost in line with the Indian economy. When we invest in an index like the SENSEX 30, we are betting on the Indian economy. If we believe that India will grow over the next 30+ years to become one of the richest countries in the world, we are getting a piece of that with indexing.

Index funds are designed to be held for the long term, which means investors can ride out market fluctuations and avoid the temptation to make emotional investment decisions during periods of market volatility.

Less Expensive

One of the key advantages of index funds is their cost-effectiveness. Index funds simply track the index without any research on companies. It simplifies operations and lowers the cost of operation. Index funds do not need many professionals researching various companies as that decision is already made by the index. They just have to keep the portfolio close to the index and buy/sell based on the money coming or going out of the fund.

Index funds are passively managed and aim to track a particular index. As a result, the expenses involved in managing the fund are relatively low compared to actively managed funds, which require more research, analysis and expertise to generate alpha (i.e., returns above a benchmark).

Index funds typically have lower expense ratios, which are the annual fees charged by fund managers to cover operating costs. In addition, because index funds trade less frequently than actively managed funds, they have lower transaction costs and incur fewer capital gains taxes.

The cost advantage of index funds is particularly important over the long term, as even small differences in expense ratios can add up to significant differences in returns. By minimizing costs, investors can keep more of their returns and compound their earnings over time, potentially leading to higher overall investment gains.

Tax Advantages

The index is evaluated at a rare frequency, such as once a year, and doesn't change very frequently. This results in a lot of tax efficiency for the fund and investors. Most of the trades in the fund are long-term, and long-term gains are lower than short-term gains. Index funds have several advantages when it comes to taxation. Some of these advantages include:

Tax Efficiency: Index funds typically have lower portfolio turnover rates than actively managed funds, which means they generate fewer taxable events, such as capital gains distributions. This can result in lower taxes for investors who hold the fund for the long term.

Lower Capital Gains Taxes: When an index fund sells a security at a profit, the gains are passed on to investors in the form of capital gains distributions. However, these gains are typically taxed at a lower rate than short-term gains, which are generated by securities held for less than one year. This is because long-term capital gains are subject to a lower tax rate than short-term capital gains.

No Capital Gains Taxes Until Sold: Investors in index funds only have to pay capital gains taxes when they sell their shares. This means that investors can hold onto their shares for as long as they want without having to worry about paying taxes on any capital gains.

Index funds are a popular investment option among investors due to their various benefits, including their tax advantages. One of the significant advantages of index funds is that there **is no minimum investment period**, allowing investors to buy and sell shares whenever they want. This flexibility is especially beneficial for investors who require liquidity.

Another advantage of index funds is **diversification**. Index funds invest in a broad range of stocks or bonds, which reduces the risk of any one stock or bond significantly affecting the fund's performance. By investing in multiple stocks or bonds, investors can spread their risk and potentially earn more consistent returns.

Furthermore, index funds provide several tax advantages. Index funds typically have lower portfolio turnover rates than actively managed funds, resulting in fewer taxable events, such as capital gains distributions. This can lead to lower taxes for investors who hold the fund for the long term. Additionally, when an index fund sells a security at a profit, the gains are typically taxed at a lower rate than short-term gains. Investors in index funds only have to pay capital gains taxes when they sell their shares, giving them more control over their tax liability.

Overall, index funds are a great option for investors looking for long-term, tax-efficient investment vehicles that offer diversification and flexibility. Investors should research and choose the right index fund that aligns with their investment goals and risk profile.

The Magic of Compounding Returns

Compounding refers to the process of earning returns on an initial investment as well as on the accumulated returns over time. In the stock market, gains do not require immediate tax payment, unlike with an FD, until the investment is sold. This means that gains in the stock market can continue to earn money for many years to come, thus helping to compound returns as the invested amount and returns continue to earn money.

For example, if you were to buy an investment that compounds for 30 years at 15% per annum, you would pay a one-time tax at the end of that period, allowing the tax amount to work for you all those years. In contrast, if you bought the same investment every year, 20% of the taxes would be paid to the government every year, reducing your investment capital and returns.

The advantages of compounding are numerous, including increasing returns, taking advantage of the time value of money, reducing transaction costs, reducing risk and increasing savings. Compounding is a powerful tool for investors, providing the potential for significant returns over time while also helping to reduce risk and minimize transaction costs.

Another benefit of indexing is that it is easy on our time and energy. Individual stocks and frequent trading require constant attention and can be emotionally taxing. Indexing allows you to invest and forget, knowing that over the long term, the market will trend upwards and you will make money along the way. Rebalancing the portfolio once a year only takes a few hours.

Moreover, passive investing using indexing takes the emotion out of investing decisions, which can often lead to bad decisions. Emotional stability is critical not to be swayed by what markets are doing or what others think. Warren Buffett even argues that an average IQ is enough for investing, but high emotional stability is essential.

Lastly, indexing has proven to be an effective way to beat the market, as evidenced by historical data from the US stock market. Despite the many mutual funds and hedge funds, no single mutual fund manager has been able to beat the index for more than ten years after considering expenses and taxes. This is why index funds have become increasingly popular among investors, providing a low-cost and reliable way to match the performance of the market indexes over the long term.

In conclusion, the magic of compounding returns and the benefits of indexing make it an excellent choice for investors looking to maximize their returns while minimizing risk and transaction costs. By investing in index funds and taking emotion out of the equation, investors can achieve greater financial security and peace of mind over the long term.

Takes Emotion Out of Investing. Not Exciting: Very Boring

Investing in the stock market can be an emotional rollercoaster. When the market is up, investors feel euphoric and confident, while a downward trend can lead to fear and panic. These emotional reactions often result in poor investment decisions, such as selling off stocks during a downturn or buying high during a market rally. This is where index funds can be a valuable tool in taking emotion out of investing.

Passive investing using indexing is very boring. It takes the emotion out of investing decisions. The worst decisions made for investing are using emotions and fear. Buffett talks about how average IQ is enough for investing but high emotional stability is super critical not to be swayed by what markets are doing or others think.

Chapter Summary/Key Takeaways: Indexing has many benefits for building wealth over the long term like diversification, monthly investment plans, tax efficiency and lower expenses. Indexing as a concept is difficult to follow due to the noise created by the Wall Street industry, media and basic human psychology. You need a deeper understanding of the concept and build your conviction by reading about the concept and experimenting to get the conviction. It is easier to understand these concepts once in our life and follow indexing for better returns than gaining knowledge for stock picking or finding the best active fund manager or an individual financial adviser.

Chapter 11:
Sounds Too Good to Be True; What Is the Catch?

I have often wondered why stock market indexing is not more popular over the past 20 years. Although I have shared this knowledge with many friends and relatives, few have taken the time to understand it and even fewer have implemented it in their lives. However, I have had success recently in sharing this knowledge with younger generations who have less than five years of work experience.

There are several main reasons why stock market indexing is not popular:

1. The financial industry thrives on selling their expertise to us and they really do not want everyone to know about index funds. They sell products with higher expense ratios promising to beat market returns. Almost all mutual fund companies have index funds, but they do not advertise them because the amount of

money they make on these funds is very limited compared to other mutual funds. It is only natural from their own business interest to not talk about index funds unless we go and ask for them. This approach pretty much takes most of the financial industry out of jobs. For their own self-interest, they will continue to come up with complex products like life insurance + investing, etc. I strongly recommend separating these with clear goals rather than combining them.

2. The media also wants to catch eyeballs by highlighting the highs and lows of the stock market. If everyone turns to index funds, there is limited interest in stock market ups and downs on a daily basis. Finance media and regular media keep giving headlines like "Market lost so many crores in two days," etc., which attract a lot of attention. In an ideal world, if the majority of investors switch to index funds, they would not pay attention to the stock market's daily swings. It would automatically reduce their ratings and revenue. This is similar to negative news in the media, which gets a lot of attention compared to some great work done by an individual somewhere in the country. They are just showing what is of interest to the common

man. It is human psychology that is a problem rather than blaming this on the media.

3. Human psychology is counter-intuitive to indexing. All of the financial industry wants us to believe that we can beat the market because it serves their purpose to grow the industry with trades and collecting fees. Most of us buy into their drumbeat that we can beat the market and we can also be a Warren Buffet. We need to understand that Warren Buffet has become popular because of his rare achievement in picking companies and making money. We need to accept that not everyone can do the same. We all want to be above average or want to be the best in everything we do. It is part of every human spirit to do better than others, which is driving the evolution of our society. Indexing is presented as or looks like, an average return of the stock market, which is totally false. At first glance, it feels like indexing is an average stock return and picking stocks or trusting an active mutual fund manager seems like a notch above to get better returns than the average stock market. This high-level understanding has two flaws in the conclusion:

a. Individual stock pickers or active fund managers can beat the index in the short term. But they are not able to beat the index over a long period of time. The index outperformed 85% of fund managers over 15 years and 99% of fund managers over 30 years in the US stock market.

b. The index is not average and it is usually picked by a group of experts in stock picking. Effectively, you are trusting the intelligence of these experts more than any active fund manager or your ability to pick stocks.

The second counter-intuitive aspect of psychology concerns timing the market. As an active trader, you may be tempted to buy more when the market is rising and sell more when it is crashing, following the crowd. Alternatively, you may feel that the market is overpriced and sell, expecting it to decline, or vice versa. The hard truth is that no one knows the market's direction. For example, the current bull run in the stock market has been going since 2008 and many tried to time the market from 2018, thinking it was too high. However, they missed the bull ride, as the market continued to rise. Every TV channel and newspaper conducts debates with experts about whether the market has peaked, but we should not base our investment decisions on those discussions.

4. To follow this concept requires a holistic understanding of it. While it may feel easier to outsource investments to mutual fund managers or brokers, there is another group of investors who are like gamblers and enjoy the thrill of the stock market's rollercoaster ride. However, for a 40+ year investment period, it is worth our time and energy to understand this philosophy fully.

5. Financial advisers have their own interests and they are often not aligned with the indexing investment model. For instance, they may recommend mutual funds from a specific company because they receive better commissions for getting customers from that company. They will not get anything for recommending an index fund from any company, as the expense ratios are low. Additionally, most financial advisers are not knowledgeable about the stock market. The charges of financial advisers for a big portfolio are very high year on year, which is entirely unnecessary. The effort you put into identifying the right financial adviser or active fund manager is equal to or more than the effort

you need to understand the indexing concept and follow it for the rest of your life.

Be fearful when others are greedy and Be greedy when others are fearful.

Financial Services and Media Sectors

The financial industry thrives on stock trading, insurance plans for investment and mutual fund management. Media thrives on attracting eyeballs with sensational news. Both drivers are opposite to indexing investment philosophy. I will not say it is a conspiracy but natural forces working against this investing philosophy.

The financial industry creates many products out of stock market equities and they charge fees for managing it. There are so many instruments and products in the market that it is easy to get confused or lost in no time. Here are a few things we keep hearing from the industry which are some versions of stock trading:

- Insurance products

- Day Trading

- Futures and Options

- Mutual funds

- Commodities trading

- ETFs

- Expert advice and newsletters for stock tips

- Personal finance advisers

The financial industry thrives on stock trading and charges for its services. They will make money either through our trades, fund charges or % of your portfolio for managing it. The point is they make money irrespective of the stock market going up or down. The industry offers many well-cooked dishes which are bad for your health. Those options are good for short-term kicks (good and bad) but not for building long-term wealth. What is required for us is a plain *daal* and rice which is indexing.

While some financial institutions offer index fund investment options, the financial industry is more focused on providing investment products that generate higher returns than the overall market through active management and stock-picking strategies. This approach involves more risk and higher fees, which can erode returns over time.

From 2003 onwards, the US mortgage industry converted a lot of mortgage loans into a complex set of products to sell to investors. It was so complex that we couldn't see the underlying asset of the product. This continued for some time and resulted in the 2007 market crash in the USA.

Similarly, the media thrives on attracting eyeballs with sensational news or market experts' advice. It feels good for us to get tips from experts and look at those companies, also believe that we also get convinced with some metrics/company balance sheet and buy them. But we need to remember that nobody in the WORLD knows where the stock market is going for the next few months. Even Warren Buffett doesn't know the 3-months-prediction of a company he invests in. He is only relying on the underlying business to make money for the company, which results in stock prices going up in the long run.

The combination of these two is a cocktail mix for a career professional. They maintain such a high noise with complex products, continued marketing on pushing mutual funds, trading. All this keeps indexing as a concept hidden in the back as it will not help them make a lot of money from investors. They either want to sell complex products with high charges or they want to run your portfolio to get a slice of that amount irrespective of returns.

Chapter Summary/Key Takeaways; Indexing is not popular as it conflicts with the interests of stock trading, the mutual fund industry and the media too. The media wants some sensation to talk about stock market swings, stock tips from pundits and round table discussions. Indexing is also counter-intuitive to human psychology. Most of us are swayed by market timing temptation, stories of our friends and relatives making money in short-term trades, etc.

Chapter 12:
Index Funds in India and Misconceptions

In India, the popularity of index funds has been growing steadily over the past few years, as more and more investors are beginning to realize their advantages over actively managed funds. Index fund assets under management (AUM) are currently 10% (Rs. 3 trillion) of the overall mutual fund AUM. They have been growing rapidly in recent years from almost 1% to 10%. They are expected to grow eight times to Rs. 25 trillion by the year 2025. In comparison, index funds account for 40% of mutual funds in the United States. In India, indexing still has a long way to go. Indexing % demonstrates the investment maturity and stability of the country and its investors.

Passive funds' AUM to grow 8-times to Rs. 25 trillion by 2025: Report - The Economic Times (indiatimes. com)

Index funds have gained significant popularity in India over the past few years. The Securities and Exchange Board of India (SEBI), which is the regulator of the securities market in India, has taken several initiatives to promote index funds in the country.

One of the major advantages of index funds in India is their low expense ratio. As compared to actively managed funds, index funds have lower management fees and operating expenses. This makes them a cost-effective investment option for retail investors.

Another advantage of index funds in India is that they offer diversification across different sectors and companies. This reduces the risk associated with investing in a single company or sector. Moreover, it also eliminates the need for investors to research individual companies and sectors, as index funds track a benchmark index.

Additionally, index funds in India also offer tax efficiency. Long-term capital gains on equity mutual funds are tax-free in India if they are held for more than one year. This means that if an investor holds an index fund for more than a year, any capital gains made on the investment will not be subject to tax.

In India, there are several options for investing in index funds. Some of the most popular index funds are the Nifty 50 Index Fund, the BSE SENSEX Index Fund and the Nifty Next 50 Index Fund. These funds are offered by several major mutual fund companies, including HDFC, ICICI Prudential and SBI Mutual Fund.

Investors in India can also choose between two types of index funds: direct and regular. Direct index funds are sold directly to investors, while regular index funds are sold through intermediaries like financial advisers or brokers. Direct index funds tend to have lower fees than regular index funds, as they do not require the same level of commission payments.

Overall, the growth of the Indian economy and the increasing participation of retail investors in the stock market have contributed to the popularity of index funds in India. With low expense ratios, diversification and tax efficiency, index funds can be a viable investment option for investors looking to build long-term wealth.

Here are the typical reasons against index funds quoted by stock market experts:

- Lack of downside protection when markets are crashing:

- o True in the short-term but no good alternative solution than going long-term as market timing is never going to work for anyone.

- Lack of Reactive Ability

  - o It is about market timing for the short term. If your stock fundamentals are right, there is no need for short-term market timing. Due to negative sentiments, stock can go down in the short term but it will bounce back in max one or two years. In fact, when the market goes down and your conviction is strong, you may want to buy more at a lower price.

- No Control Over Holdings

  - o A group of experts is picking the stocks for you. You are depending on this group of experts rather than your time/expertise to pick stocks. For making money in the long term, this works. But if you want to experience this yourself, you can play with a small amount by buying stocks individually.

- Single Strategy

- o Simple and Single strategy which works. If goals are aligned in terms of making money in the long term, this should not matter.

- No Personal Satisfaction

  - o Investing money is different from satisfaction or control. The single goal of investment is to make money in the long run with less effort. If it means less engagement and less control, so be it.

- Buying companies at an early stage by active fund managers for better reruns before they are added to the index.

  - o There are many examples recently where companies started crashing after listing them on the stock market. A good example is PayTM. You would have lost a lot of money if you invested in PayTM before listing it on the stock market.

  - o The benefit of buying a stock before adding to the stock index is limited but risks are high. The whole point is about buying the stock in the index. What if a stock you bought thinking that it would be added to the index was never added to it? It will be very challenging to manage and track the index and I am sure all active funds managers are doing it now or in previous years but they were not successful in the long run.

- Buy the top 10 stocks and forget it

  o Self-cleaning process of the index to add or remove new companies to our investment portfolio over the long term. The stock market was dominated by steel and auto in the 70s, finance and oil companies in the 80s and health and internet in the 90s. GM, GE, IBM, US Steel, AT&R, ExxonMobil and Microsoft are examples of top companies in their areas but not a single company stayed in the top five most valuable companies throughout. The pace of change is only increasing with technology, and it is not possible for any single individual to stay on top of these new trends for investments.

If you notice, most of them are true in the short term and for personal experience of picking stocks. But the fundamental question is, are we investing for the short term or long term? If your goal is to achieve higher returns over the long term, none of these arguments holds true.

Stock market and financial industry professionals make it complex either intentionally or unintentionally for the common man so that they can play a role in helping the common man and start charging fees.

Chapter Summary/Key Takeaways: Stock market indexing is not well-known in India and it is still at a very early stage. There are many conceptions spread by the media and the finance industry and it is in their interest to keep this below visibility to sell their services and complex products to the common man.

Part IV:
Investing Simplified By Life Stage

Investing by life stage or age is an important concept in financial planning. The approach to investing varies depending on the individual's goals, risk tolerance and financial position, which often change as one progresses through different stages of life.

In the early stages of life, individuals usually have less financial responsibility and more time to invest, making it an opportune time to start investing. During this stage, the focus should be on building a strong foundation for future financial stability. As such, one can take more risks and invest in higher-risk assets such as stocks, mutual funds, or Exchange-Traded Funds (ETFs) to take advantage of their potential for higher returns over time.

However, in the mid-career stage, the focus shifts to long-term financial goals such as retirement planning, paying for children's education, or buying a home. At this stage, an individual's financial position may improve, which can allow for a more diversified investment portfolio with a mix of lower-risk and higher-risk assets. A balanced investment approach can help to protect against market fluctuations while still offering the potential for growth.

In the later stages of life, the focus shifts towards preserving the wealth accumulated over the years and generating a stable stream of income. At this stage, investment strategies should prioritize safety and stability, which often means shifting towards lower-risk investments such as bonds or fixed deposits. These investments provide steady, predictable returns and help to protect against market volatility.

Regardless of age or life stage, it is important to have a well-diversified portfolio. This means spreading investments across a variety of asset classes such as stocks, bonds, real estate and cash. Diversification helps to mitigate risk and ensure a steady return on investment, regardless of market conditions.

This part of the book covers investment strategies and vehicles based on your life stage. This part is divided into three chapters to cover various stages of life for achieving financial independence:

1. The early stage of a career begins with small investments to accumulate wealth by saving small amounts every month,

2. The growing stage is about investments which can be leveraged to grow wealth with a balance of risk, and

3. The stabilizing stage is about stabilizing assets with an investment strategy focused on protecting the principal with yields paying for your retirement life. We will also talk about a use case on how it can possibly pan out with these investment strategies.

Chapter 13: STARTING STAGE (21 to 35) – Investing in Early Stages of Career.

After finishing college, either through campus recruitment or efforts outside campus, you finally land a job. It is a great experience to earn and spend your own money. For the first time, you get a pay cheque for the time and energy you spend working for a company. This is also the time of life when your expenses are the lowest in your life as you will be staying in some form of shared accommodation and without any financial commitments like loans for a car or house. All savings during this time will have the longest duration to multiply the investment. But it is also the time when we will not have the financial understanding to invest. I spoke to many senior employees over the years and many of them repent having missed the opportunity to save money during this phase. Even if we want to save money during this time, we do not know where to start. Another big challenge is that the amounts available are too small to invest in areas like real estate. Basically, we have three challenges as career professionals during this phase:

1. Value of Saving Early – We do not understand the value of saving early and compounding earnings over time

2. Where to Start – We are not aware of financial investment options and starting point

3. Small Saving Amounts – The investable amount is small and end up spending most of the salary

We will discuss each of these challenges, options and steps to take during this phase of the career.

1. **Value of Saving Early**

   As you start your employment and start getting a monthly salary, you want to enjoy the freedom and money with your friends and family. It is well-deserved for all the hard work you put into your college and landing a job. After the initial few months of enjoying this phase, it is important to set up goals for saving and investing. This is the phase where we miss the biggest opportunity to save early and compound over time. Money saved during the early stage of life gives you returns like no other time. To highlight the impact of this, please see the example below with two scenarios:

Scenario 1: Ram saved 1 lakh per year from age 21 to 35 (Total 15L saved by Ram) and left that amount till age 65

Scenario 2: Ram did not figure out the savings early. He realized later and saved 1 lakh per year from age 35 to 65(Total 30L saved by Ram)

Assuming a 10% return, can you calculate the final balance of Ram's savings at age 65 in these two scenarios?

It is 40+ cr for scenario 1 and 5+ crores in scenario 2.

Observe the contrast of the final amount at age 65 though Ram saved double the money in the second scenario. We are assuming 10% returns for both scenarios.

It is extremely important to save early and leave it invested over a long term to get the compound effect by letting your money work for you.

Govt. collects 10% to 38% tax on your income every month. You don't see that money in your account at all. You don't really miss it either. You plan your spending or expenses based on what is deposited into your account. With the same mindset, you need to save every month a % of money deposited into your salary account.

Action: Think of 10 to 15% of your salary as a tax you are paying to yourself for the later stage of life.

2. **Where to Start**

Now that we understand the importance of saving early, the next question is where to start: fixed deposit (FD), real estate, stock market, gold, etc. We will look at each of these options to understand the pros and cons at this stage of life.

Fixed Deposits

In the absence of a proper understanding of investments, many of us start with FDs as that is the safest option as learned from our parents. It worked to some extent for our parent generation with higher interest rates but it is not working now. One of the reasons is the economic liberalization that started in the 1990s. Interest rates are low and inflation is high over the last three decades. Yes…, it is the safest option to protect your money but not a good option to grow your money. Here are two main challenges with FDs:

- FD returns are always less than inflation. What this means is the value of your money is actually going down with time due to inflation. If you can buy 1 kg of rice with your money today, you will not be able to buy the same quantity of rice five years later with returns from FDs, because the price of rice will go up more than your returns due to inflation.

- The interest you earn on FDs is taxed every year along with your income. For example, if you are in the higher tax bracket of 33% due to your salary income, your FD interest income is taxed every year at the same rate. It means 1/3 of your FD income is going as tax at the year-end.

- Tax is paid every year in FDs while **tax is paid only when you sell in the case of stocks or real estate**. It means that the tax you paid in year-1 will continue to work for you to make more money if you stay invested for the next 30 years.

This is a big multiplier over the long term in stocks and real estate.

Real Estate

There are many good stories you hear about people making a lot of money in real estate in some parts of the country. It is true that big money is being made in real estate by many. Here are two challenges at the beginning of the career to start investing in real estate:

1. The amount required to invest in real estate is typically high like a minimum of 10L to sometimes crores. As someone starting out in his career, it is very challenging to save the amount required to buy real estate. In addition, you also need a good understanding of the real estate market in your city and you have to buy the property at a single point in time. It means you must commit all your investments at the same time. If the prices are at a peak and start crashing, there are limited mitigation strategies to avoid losses.

2. It is cyclical with a long-term horizon. Some of the markets like Mumbai went down or did not grow even for a decade. Unfortunately, you cannot buy real estate across the country but you

will end up localized to a city or an area within the city. For example, the Hyderabad real estate market has been doing extremely well for the last six years but it was down for more than a decade before that. There are areas in Hyderabad like Shamshabad which went down in 2007 and started recovering only in 2017. 10-year return on those investments was zero or negative.

3. Due diligence and maintaining the safety of the property – You need to do a lot of due diligence to ensure that property title/ownership is legitimate. You also need to spend time to maintain the safety of the property.

4. Liquidity: It is also not available as cash or stocks in crisis. If you have a crisis, you can't sell the real estate property as you need to find a buyer in the market to pay a reasonable market price.

Stock Market

As we discussed in Chapter III, the stock market offers an opportunity to buy stocks in public business at market price. As the business grows, your investment grows with the business. For example, if you own a % of a Reliance company, your investment grows along with Reliance company valuation, or you can even say, along with Mukesh Ambani's wealth. The difference is in the % ownership of the company. As the Indian economy is growing, there are multitudes of these businesses that created wealth for shareholders over the last three decades and they will continue to create a lot of wealth for the next three decades. Most of the wealthy in the country like Tatas, Birlas, Ambanis and Adanis are rich from the stock market valuations of their companies. Mukesh Ambani is one of the richest in the world because of the stock wealth created by Reliance company and that is reflected in the India stock market opportunity along with the economy.

Historical returns of the Indian stock market show that for any five-year period from 1979 to till date, SENSEX returned positive returns 34 times out of 37 (1984–2021) and only three times negative returns of your investment. If you take a 10-year return, it never returned negative returns. **SENSEX's 30-year average return is 15% per year. It means 1L (8333 per month) invested consistently through SIPS every month in the SENSEX index without worrying/changing plans with up or down market from 1992 to till date, would have accumulated a sum of around six crores as of today. If you leave it without further investment for another 10 years, it is expected to be 20+ crores.**

I understand that it may not be practical to exactly follow this path due to unexpected expenses and errors in human judgement, etc. But this highlights the opportunity in the stock market without the noise of media and stock picking advice, etc. This approach is not exciting at all in the short term as you can't boast of huge returns like others about making big money but it really works in the long term.

It may be difficult to get started with this approach and build the initial five years of execution due to smaller amounts of investment and limited returns but later it will become very visible. I strongly recommend not to dip into this account for every-day needs but you can always use this account for some planned expenses. For example, by adding 1L every year with 15% expected returns, you will have around 10L at the end of 5 years. You can always leverage 2L from this account to buy your first car down payment. Similarly, after 10 years, you are expected to have 30L in this account. You can leverage 10L from this balance to pay the advance amount for your first apartment. You need to be sure about the real need of the purchase and be aware that you are reducing the final retirement amount by a very big amount by taking money from this account. If they are genuine necessities and not luxury items, you are ok to do that.

Assuming you start your savings at age 21 and you take these two expenses and start investing 10K per month at a 7% increment in savings for each in line with the increase in your salary, you will end up with a **7.8 crore balance by the age of 51, and 30 crores by age 60**. I want to highlight that this is not the limit to your wealth creation. It is the foundation of your wealth creation, and you can always experiment with local real estate with money saved in addition to this amount. But they are unpredictable and sometimes you make money in a short time. Once this foundation is set, you can afford to take those calculated risks to make more money with short-term returns.

3. **Small Saving Amounts**

> As the amounts are small early in your career, it feels like you can't invest small amounts anywhere and you end up spending most of the money. But we need to understand that the longest journey starts with a first step. It is important to initiate that first step towards wealth to achieve financial independence. The stock market gives you that opportunity to invest small amounts every month with risk-free options in the long term.

Consider a 10K per month investment into the stock market every month as you start your career. It is not difficult for anyone making 50K per month. If your salary is around 25K per month, you can consider Rs. 5000 savings per month. An important point is to save a % of your salary every month and put it into the stock market to build wealth long-term.

During our initial career days, this is the best investment option considering the simplicity of investing in an index, small monthly amounts and risk profile. After five years of doing this assuming a 10% increment in your salary and savings, you are looking at a 10L portfolio which will be a good starting point to build your long-term wealth.

To summarize, you will build a foundation during the first 15 years of your career with small saving amounts every month by putting them into the stock market index. Along the way, you will probably buy a car and home which you can dip into this savings. Assuming 10K savings per month with a 7% increase in savings, 15% annual return and 2L & 10L used for car (around 24 years) and home (around 30 years), you will be sitting on a stock market index savings of around 70 lakhs. During this time, we have assumed your savings per year going from 10K per month to 27.5K per month increasing only 7% per year. We have assumed lower % savings due to higher expenses and taxes over your life journey from age 21 to 35.

Chapter Summary/Key Takeaways: At the beginning of your career, it is best to start investing in stock market indexing maintaining the discipline of contributions every month. Fixed deposits (FDs) are the least preferred due to lower returns and high taxes. Real estate is not possible as the amount you have is not suited for a single bulk amount investment. Set up a Systematic Investment Plan (SIP) every month to automatically buy index funds in the stock market. As you continue to accumulate and compound your savings, you need to commit for at least 5+ years commitment to stay invested.

After you start stock market indexing with SIPs, you can continue to research other investment options like real estate to understand them better. That will help you to invest after you accumulate good amounts using stock market indexing.

<u>ACTION</u>: Open a mutual fund account either with HDFC or ICICI (it is available as a folder in your HDFC bank account which needs to be enabled) and set up a weekly or monthly Systematic Investment Plan (SIP) to buy any of the index funds. Here are the names of index funds in HDFC: HDFC INDEX FUND - SENSEX PLAN & HDFC Index Fund - Nifty 50 Plan GR. You can go with either of them.

Chapter 14:
GROWING STAGE
(36 to 50) – Investing in
Mid-career

We will discuss alternate investments which can be explored during this phase of life in addition to the stock market indexing. This is not about moving out of stock market indexing to invest in other areas. This is about continuing the stock market indexing and also leveraging short-term growth opportunities in areas like real estate now that you have the amounts required to start investing in real estate. This chapter will mainly focus on real estate investment options and how to decide on them. This is on top of stock market indexing which is the foundational investment for everyone.

During this phase of life, you get busy with more responsibilities at work and personal life. It is also the phase where the expenses will increase drastically with kids' school education and a bigger home to support the family. You are stretched in many directions with very limited time to balance work and life. By this time, you would have hopefully researched other investment options like real estate. Real estate is not a simple straightforward investment like stock market indexing. You did not require any knowledge about a company, business model, growth opportunities, etc. Index did that for you by picking the top 30 or 50 companies representing the Indian economy. It is important to understand this difference as it comes with its own risks and rewards. This is the reason, we can bet a small portion of our wealth on real estate but stock market indexing still has to be the foundation of investment strategy. For example, if you have accumulated a crore in stock market indexing, you can't take that amount and put it into real estate. It is a huge mistake. You can think of taking a small percentage like 20% and use that money to try your luck in real estate. If you make a proper investment, you may get higher returns on this investment in the short term like five years when you sell and buy another real estate property.

The best thing about indexing is having zero knowledge of stocks or companies and blindly trusting a group of experts who picked the index. It also goes through a self-cleansing process where companies get dropped or added to the index based on expert opinions. Your investment automatically tracks those changes and comes out as the winner in the end. Unfortunately, you do not have that option in real estate. You need to do proper research to find areas of the city which are expected to grow and provide better rental values. The great thing about real estate is that it is only growing in the long term of 10+ years. The simple reason is the limited land and growing population. Indexing also provides this automatic protection as it continues to grow along with the Indian economy.

When you are looking for real estate investment, you need to decide on two options: Monthly rental (yield) vs. Growth.

In general, growth returns are higher compared to rental returns. But rental returns give you that safety net of replacing your salary income at some point. I strongly recommend growth opportunities during this phase of life. During the next phase of life 50+, you can plan on converting these growth investments to yield investments for replacing salary with fixed income.

Options for growth are individual plots, apartments and villas in upcoming areas. There are many examples of our parents' generation investing in a small plot with small amounts which is very valuable now.

Identifying the location of the investment is the most important decision for real estate. There is a saying that the top three things to consider for real estate investment are LOCATION, LOCATION and LOCATION ☺

That explains the importance of location in real estate. It is about the area of the city and the exact location of your investment. You need to start thinking of upcoming growth areas of the city. **It depends on the following three points:**

1. Proximity to the existing central business district or new business area announced by govt.: As the Indian economy is growing, there are new areas of growth clusters announced by govt. from time to time. There is a risk of hype with this and it is important to invest at the beginning of the cycle.

2. Infrastructure being developed by the government in that area: If it is a new area, you do need to look for basic infrastructure to be provided by govt. with roads. It is a signal of govt. support and plan for that area. If it is adjacent to the existing business district, it is important to check out the roads connecting this new area to the central business district.

3. Price of the property: The price of the property is one of the most important factors for investment. If the prices are already high and baked in for future growth, there is limited opportunity for your investment to grow.

Of these three investment options for growth, I really like villas for multiple reasons. Please do understand that each of them has its pros and cons. You need to evaluate your risk-taking ability to decide on the investment:

1. **Plot**: It is the most popular investment with many of our parents' generation and continues to be popular with many even now. Plots are relatively safe as they have gone through govt. approval. Also, it offers plots of all sizes starting from 150 sq. Yds to 1000 sq. Yd and you can find the plot that fits your investment amount and needs. The plot will be immediately registered in your name and you can leave it for a few years for the value to appreciate. A disadvantage of the plot is its usability. For too long, plots will keep changing hands with an increase in value but people constructing homes take a lot of time. Another challenge is a feeling of community. There is no uniform time when everyone comes together. One individual will construct his home

today while the whole community will take 5+ years to construct and start living in the area.

2. **Apartment:** Apartment is another good option leveraged by many. This investment is a combination of growth and rental returns. If you invest during the early phase of the project, you will make the payments at a slower pace and the apartment's value starts going up as the project gets to the completion stage. At this point, you can decide to sell to get growth returns or keep to rent out the apartment for rental returns. The builder is adding value to the property by constructing the building. The good thing about an apartment is that it is usable for someone and delivers value at the end of it, unlike plots. One disadvantage of apartments is that the growth is limited compared to plots. The land value of areas is growing faster and the land share of apartments is very limited.

3. **Villa:** Villa investment has the combined advantages of a plot and an apartment. It grows faster as there is a decent land portion and the builder adds value by constructing the community. It is a group of plots where a builder is constructing all homes at the same time and

providing the social infrastructure for families to move in at the end of the project. In addition, you have the luxury of reserving a villa with an initial small amount and paying the rest of the amount as per the development progress. Villa projects also take too much time to complete and typically it is four years. As a salary holder with a fixed income, it is a lot easier to pay for them with small amounts over the years apart from loans. It works really well for career professionals. They do appreciate much and your returns are very high in comparison to the amounts invested by you.

EXIT STRATEGY IN REAL ESTATE: Most real estate investments go through a hyper-growth time and then stabilize for very long periods. This is different from stock market indexing where you are keeping the investment for life.

Indexing vs. Real Estate

Real estate investment is very popular for many while indexing is not as much. There are many popular guys who became rich with real estate but we do not hear about the popular rich guys talking about indexing. Both real estate and indexing have their own pros and cons and both have their place in your investment strategy based on your stage of life, risk-taking ability and lifestyle. It is important to understand these pros and cons to make the right decision on our investments.

Indexing

As we learned through the book, indexing is not popular. It is honest and boring at best as it doesn't require your time and brains. But they are highly diversified, less risky and of low cost. A typical expense ratio of index funds is 0.1% compared to 1% in active mutual funds. You do not need a professional portfolio manager as it is Do-It-Yourself (DIY) with very little time.

One downside with indexing is you are at the mercy of market swings but it is not a big deal if you are in for the long run as you ride them out over a period.

Real Estate Investing

A big advantage of real estate is monthly rental income to cover the mortgage. It feels good to get a monthly income just like a salary without any sweat. It makes you feel better and you can use these earnings to invest to build wealth.

The second biggest advantage is the ability to use leverage. If you pay a 20% down payment for a property, you can get a loan for 80%. For example, if you buy a property for 1cr, you can invest 20L from your savings and get a loan for 80L. You are leveraging an 80L loan and investing in a property worth 1cr. When the property appreciates, your equity increases not only for your savings but also for the loan amount. For example, a 10% increase in the property is equal to 10L which is a 50% return on your savings investment of 20L. Returns are much higher in real estate due to leveraging but we need to be aware of downside risks too in case of real estate pricing going down.

You can improve the property value with sweat contribution. You can renovate with sweat and increase property value which is not possible in indexing.

Downsides

> Real estate investment requires a lot of hands-on activity. If you are busy with your profession and life, it takes a toll on the amount of time required to manage the property, renters and repairs.

Real estate is location-dependent with high risk. You are tied to a location or property for your 1cr investment. Your returns highly depend on picking the right location. Otherwise, it will be a huge issue managing a property going down in value.

It requires a lot of upfront cash. You need at least 20% down which means typically 20L for a 1cr investment or 10L for a 50L investment, whereas you can start an index investment with a simple Rs. 100 and start the SIP with a minimum Rs.100. During the initial stage of your career, it makes absolute sense to get started with indexing to start accumulating lakhs before thinking of real estate. During this phase of life at 36+, you will have a balance of 10L+ to start thinking about real estate investment.

Your investment in real estate is not liquid cash. You can't get cash in case of emergencies as you need to find a buyer to sell the property. Sometimes it takes months to find a buyer and get cash into the hand. In the case of index funds, it is just a click of a button and you will have cash in your account in a couple of working days max.

<u>Other Alternate Assets:</u> There are many other alternate asset investments like commodities, insurance, foreign currency, etc. But I am not going to get into details of these.

I strongly believe it is not important to understand all the options but to master limited investment options and leverage them well. I want to avoid confusion with too many investment options and really focus on stock market indexing and real estate to build your long-term wealth. Of these two, stock market indexing doesn't require any knowledge, time and effort while real estate does require you to understand, decide and spend time to buy and manage property.

Chapter Summary/Key Takeaways: Mid-career, now that you accumulated some decent amounts, it is time to take some calculated risks to participate in hyper-growth real estate areas. It is very important to not switch from stock market indexing to real estate but only take a small % to get into real estate. It comes with its own risks but in comparison to individual company stock, real estate is better to retain the investment over time.

We explored three options for investing with the pros and cons of each. Location is the most important element of the real estate investment decision. Also, have a clear exit strategy after hyper-growth to invest in the next hyper-growth area.

Chapter 15:
STABILIZING and Retirement STAGE (51+) – Investing in Later Stage

By this time, you have accumulated good wealth and the most important point of this life stage is protecting your wealth, generating a fixed monthly income to meet your lifestyle and continue to grow your wealth with lower risk.

<u>Stock Market Indexing wealth:</u> It is time to start thinking about a balanced portfolio and add bonds and cash to the portfolio. One rule of thumb suggested by professionals is to have bonds the same percentage as your age. It means, for example, if your age is 50 you need to have 50% in bonds/cash and the remaining in stocks. Assuming that you can still stay in the market for more than 10 years, I suggest a more aggressive approach. You can continue a majorly stock portfolio until 60 years and start moving from stocks to bonds from 60 by adding 10% bonds every year. It means you will be in 100% bonds by the age of 70.

This is the time when you can also put money in fixed deposits (FDs) which was an absolutely incorrect investment when starting at 21. There are three reasons again for suggesting this:

1. Your salary income has stopped, and you are in a lower tax bracket.

2. You don't have time on your side to take risks in the stock market and need a safe haven.

3. You need a fixed monthly income source to support your lifestyle.

<u>Real Estate Wealth:</u> Till now, you have been following the growth to make more money than stock market indexing by leveraging your local city growth areas. It is using either plots, apartments, or villas. As you get into 50+ years, it is time to reduce the risk and focus on generating monthly income to support your lifestyle. We will explore three possible options in real estate to do this and understand the pros and cons of each option:

1. **Apartments for rental:** This is the standard and most used approach as the ticket size is small. If you invested in apartments earlier for growth, it is time to think about keeping them with you

for a rental return instead of selling them for growth. Apartment rental returns are usually very low in the range of 3 to 4%. This is the most used option for many investors. Usually, smaller apartments will give better returns compared to bigger apartments but it all depends on the community, quality, interiors, etc.

PROS: Small ticket size, many options available at various levels.

CONS: You will do interiors and sometimes furnish to get a higher return on the unit. This is a problem as the tenant can damage or not maintain the unit which will result in damage to the interior work. When the tenant changes, you will end up fixing/redoing the interior which will take away a part of your returns. It is advisable to rent without interiors but difficult to find tenants in this model.

2. **Grade B or Grade C Commercial Rental:** This is a unit fully controlled by the buyer like a small shutter on a busy road or an office unit in a multi-storeyed building which can be rented or operated independently by individual business owners for their retail or office. These are typically single buildings with three to five

floors and each floor will have two to three units which can be locked separately. These units give better rental returns like 6–8% and they are also available in all sizes starting from 1 crore+. They offer complete control of our unit and require only basic operational maintenance.

PROS: Medium ticket size and many options.

CONS: Most of the time you can rent with a base shell or warm shell with very limited interiors like flooring and false roof. Businesses will do their own interior to fit their office layout needs or branding needs. This really helps improve the returns and also when there is a tenant change, offices or businesses can't effectively take all the work done in our unit. We will end up retaining some interior for free or marginal cost which will help us improve our rent with the next tenant.

3. **Grade A Commercial Rental:** This is typically 20+ floors big office building or mall. They are mostly available with big ticket sizes like 5 crore+ and mostly they are not suggested for us. Options available in smaller sizes are not recommended as most big businesses like Accenture or Wipro don't prefer buildings with multiple tenants. I strongly recommend against investing in these

units unless you can afford a complete floor of 20K sq. Ft space which will cost around 20 crores.

PROS: Zero maintenance as the building will be owned and maintained by the tenant.

CONS: Big ticket size and renting options are limited for multi-owner properties.

Chapter Summary/Key Takeaways: At the end of your career, you have accumulated wealth and it is the phase where you have the freedom to quit your job and do something new in life. You are not tied to a monthly pay cheque and you need to leverage the wealth accumulated over time to give you yield returns to cover monthly expenses. We explored multiple options in real estate.

Overall, this life stage is directional and it is up to you how to approach it now that you have achieved financial independence. You can continue to invest in growth areas and build more wealth for 60+ while you continue to work and live on your salary. Or you can convert the assets into monthly yields to quit your salary job and explore something new in life.

Epilogue/Conclusion

It is not difficult to create wealth over the long term if you have the intention, clarity, and purpose. Most of us have successful careers with a steady stream of income in our prime working duration. We need to save that income and invest consistently in stock market indexing to build wealth.

Most of us don't do it because of the clutter of information that is around us which will confuse us to the core. We get the impression that we need to understand a lot more before we can start investing and we don't get time in our busy professional lives.

The objective of this book was to simplify investing and get you started without a lot of knowledge and time. If you can get started with an initial investment and automatic SIP in an index fund, I consider it a success for this book. Please understand that it is a long journey, and you adjust your investment strategies as you get a deeper understanding of other assets like real estate, or retirement planning to achieve financial freedom. I have been doing this for the last 20+ years and worked with many young professionals and got them on this path.

Look forward to your financial investment journey/ success and hearing back from you with questions or feedback… THANK YOU for your time and wish you all the best.

Acknowledgements

Samba Nadella for introducing me to stock market indexing back in 2001.

Srini Khanna, Narasa Pekety for constant encouragement and help with overall structure.

Anitha, Shravya, Mansi, and Sahithi for proof reading and feedback as first readers.

Sriya for creating the cover design and working on multiple rounds of changes.

About the Author

 Jagan comes from a humble background with limited or no exposure to financial education in the family. He did his Computer Science engineering and is currently working as a Senior Director with Microsoft. He has global consulting experience working in the US with multiple clients as an entrepreneur.

He has been investing in Indian startups as an Angel Investor since 2011 in companies like WowMomos, GetMyParking, FreshWorld and GoCoop. He lost money in the 2000 dotcom crash in the USA and started fresh with a clear investment strategy using stock market indexing to build long-term wealth from 2002 to till date.

He lives with his wife Anitha and daughters Sahithi & Sriya in Hyderabad. As a family, they love to travel and enjoy the destinations of nature.

www.ingramcontent.com/pod-product-compliance
Lightning Source LLC
Chambersburg PA
CBHW032019140726
47988CB00017BA/556